Carry

for Revival

By Rodney Burton

with

Tom Stamman

Published by CreateSpace Independent Publishing Platform.

This title is also available as an ebook. Visit www.amazon.com

Contributors: Rodney Burton & Tom Stamman
Editors: Rodney Burton, Tom Stamman, Kim Burton, & Molly Nolden.
Cover design: Rodney Burton
Cover Artwork: Public Domain photo and CreateSpace template.
First Printing 2013
Printed in the United States of America

ISBN-13: **978-1479365326**
ISBN-10: **1479365327**

All Bible verses are the "New American Standard" version of the Bible unless otherwise noted.

All personal stories and use of the word "I" refer to Rodney Burton unless otherwise noted.

Dedication

To our wonderful Lord and Savior Jesus Christ who is not only the inspiration for this book, but the inspiration for our lives.

To our wonderful families who give us the strength, courage, and encouragement to keep going, no matter how difficult things may seem or become.

To the hearts that are hungry to experience revival in their lives, in their families, in their churches, in their communities, in their nation, and in their world.

To the wonderful men and women who carry the torch for revival. May that torch be ignited by a fresh fire from Heaven and cause a glorious combustion in the world in which you live – bringing a mighty revival to life.

About the Authors

Rodney Burton, along with his wife Kim and son Josiah, currently serve as lead pastors of Calvary Church in Carthage, Illinois. Rodney and Kim are graduates of the Brownsville Revival School of Ministry in Pensacola, Florida. Rodney is credentialed with the Assemblies of God. Their heart is to see the church come alive with the power, presence and fullness of God. They feel the church has been living far below her potential and is in great need of a mighty move of God. Rodney's preaching and writing is built around and driven by this passionate belief. You can learn more about the Burtons by visiting www.rodneyburton.net or their church website www.calvarychurchag.com.

Tom Stamman and his wife Teresa serve as Presidents of Impact Ministries International. IMI was founded in 1986, and this ministry is devoted to winning the lost to Jesus. Tom travels and speaks nearly 400 times per year, releasing prophetic words over people, equipping the church to evangelize and to be trained in the gifts of the Spirit. Tom and Teresa's motivation is to feed the poor and to plant churches. IMI currently has orphanages in fourteen countries of the world, feeding 10,000 orphans per month. To find out more information about the Stammans, IMI or their orphanages you can visit www.tstamman.com.

Table of Contents

Foreword

Thirty years ago when I was attending North Central Bible College in Minneapolis, Minnesota, I was required to write a paper on the great revivals in the Bible. I chose the story of the young King Josiah. For over thirty years, there has been a hunger for revival in my heart for the church of Jesus Christ.

What an opportunity to connect two disciples of two different revivals from two different generations. I, Rev. Tom Stamman, saved in Catholic and Lutheran Charismatic movement - teaming up to write a book with Rev. Rodney Burton, a product of the Brownsville Revival in Pensacola, Florida.

God put on my heart to write a book about revival with Pastor Rodney in 2012. The success of Josiah in his day inspires me to believe God for a revival in this generation. As you read this book, I trust that the flames of revival will burn away the layers of carnality, and thrust you into the presence of a holy God. I am honored to work together with a young man who is sold out to Jesus, and loves revival as much as anyone I have ever met. May God do it again in this generation. Open up your heart, and let God strike the match of His love, and create a fire that will last until the second coming of Christ.

Rev. Tom Stamman
Impact Ministries International

Introduction

Destiny is defined as "a person's preordained future; or the apparently predetermined and inevitable series of events that happen to somebody or something" (Encarta Dictionary: English). When a person comes into his place of destiny, something very powerful and supernatural takes place. A person who understands his destiny is often ready and willing to go to great lengths to realize that destiny.

At the tender age of eight years old, Josiah was placed on the throne as king in Jerusalem. Josiah assumed the throne at a very dark and difficult time in the history of the nation. The people whom God had set apart as His own had moved so far away from His plans and purposes for their lives. The prophets Jeremiah and Zephaniah prophesied during the time of Josiah's reign, and we can gain some insight into the condition of the times from their writings, with the words in the first chapter of Zephaniah being a great example.

"I will completely remove all things from the face of the earth," declares the Lord. "I will remove man and beast, I will remove the birds of the sky and the fish of the see, and the ruins along with the wicked; and I will cut off man from the face of the earth," declares the Lord. Zephaniah 1:2-3

Without question, the Lord was angry, and Josiah was stepping into a place of authority at this strategic point in history. What a heavy mandate and destiny that was given to young Josiah. And we find that during his thirty-one year reign he did what was right in the eyes of the Lord and led a great revival in the land (see 2 Chronicles 34). In this book we will explore the elements of that revival and how we can apply those elements within the context of the revival I know God desires to bring today. In his book, *The End of the American Gospel Enterprise,* Dr. Michael Brown describes revival in this manner:

A true revival is absolutely supernatural in its workings. It is totally God-glorifying in its character. No flesh can boast in its presence. It can not be produced, manufactured, or worked up. It is poured out, poured on, and poured in, a deluge of God from heaven. It carries all things along on the crest of its waves; it is driven by the wind of the Spirit.
(Brown, 1993, p. 35).

Josiah did not plan the revival he experienced, but he did step into God's prophetic destiny for his life (see 1 Kings 13:1-3). God had put into motion His plan to bring His people back to Himself; Josiah had the privilege of being an integral part of that plan. During his reign and during the days of this great revival, Josiah had to learn to navigate through what God was doing. While we cannot plan for or produce revival, when it comes we do have a responsibility and a role to play in it. Through this book, I hope that together we can discover a few elements of our responsibility.

I have been blessed of God to be a part of some great moves of His Spirit in a short amount of time. I was born again during revival; I accepted God's calling to ministry during revival; and my wife and I were trained for ministry at the Brownsville Revival School of Ministry in Pensacola, Florida. I do not consider myself a revival expert. I do know, however, that I carry in my heart a torch for revival. I long and hunger for a mighty outpouring of God's Spirit once again. My prayer is that together we can fan the flame (2 Timothy 1:6) of revival in our hearts and see God do what only He can do in and through our lives. Together let's see our destiny become our reality.

Chapter 1 – Stepping into Destiny

Josiah was eight years old when he became king, and he reigned thirty-one years in Jerusalem. 2 Chronicles 34:1

The Prophetic Destiny of the Brownsville Revival

On Father's Day, 1995, God opened the doorway to destiny during the Sunday morning service at Brownsville Assembly of God in Pensacola, Florida. From that moment, God sent a powerful revival that saw countless thousands of people commit their lives to the Lord and literally brought the world to the doorsteps of Brownsville. It was such a sovereign move of God that no matter how hard you try, it simply cannot be explained or fully understood. Not everyone, however, realizes the prophetic destiny that was established years before the revival began on Father's Day 1995.

In 1979 Pastor Ken Sumrall delivered a prophecy at Liberty Church, the nondenominational church he founded in Pensacola. It said of the coming revival:

"Time will be forgotten as meetings will last for hours...There will be much weeping and sobbing as sin is seen as exceedingly sinful...Youth, even the very young, will be drunk with new wine and burn with fervor, oblivious to anything and everything but obedience to Jesus...Prayer will be the main event of the church. Hundreds will be converted. Be prepared to baptize two hundred new believers at one service."

In 1997, this same Liberty Church location became the site of and the campus for the Brownsville Revival School of Ministry where hundreds of men and women were trained and instructed in ministry and revival. In December of 1999 my wife and I were part of the third graduating class of this school. We were living in the midst of fulfilled destiny.

A second documented prophecy was given in Phoenix, Arizona, by Visionaries International leader Michial Ratliff. In November 1989 Ratliff prophesied:

"Transformation will come. Many people in peril, in dire straits, will be saved dramatically. Healings will take place. Deliverances will take place. And one church in particular will humble its heart and receive Me. The college people, the students, the high schools, various people will be reckoned with by the angels of God that are loosed. This is a victory against all contempt that is stirring in the city, actually disarming the time bomb that is ticking away in Pensacola, Florida. You shall see the turnaround, and nationally will the church hear about the revival that sparked in Pensacola."

Perhaps the most well-known prophetic word given about Pensacola came from David Yonggi Cho. In 1991, Cho had a vision of America and began to hear God speak about a move of God He was going to send. Prompted by the Spirit, Cho pulled out a map of America and his finger rested in the Florida panhandle. The word of the Lord flooded his heart.

"I am going to send revival to the seaside city of Pensacola, and it will spread like a fire until all of America has been consumed by it."

I will continue to weave stories from my own life and experiences from the Brownsville Revival throughout this book. I do not, however, just want this to be a historical recollection. I pray that together we fan the flame of destiny in each and every heart. There are powerful destinies yet to be fulfilled and yours is one of them.

A Nation Becomes Ripe for Revival

It was the greatest split in recorded history. Rehoboam had taken his place on the throne in succession of his father, Solomon. Against conventional wisdom, he declared that he would serve with more control and domination and it brought about a division in the kingdom. Typically, when someone desires to establish or make a name for themselves there are many others who have to deal with the consequences.

Although guilty of bringing about the split of the kingdom, Rehoboam was still the rightful heir and of the house of David – God's established family of royalty. Doors of deception and destruction were opened because God's people were going against God's established plan. Any time an individual, a group, or even a nation works in opposition to God's plan, they are opening themselves up to the hell with which they are partnering. The resulting sin and consequence that accompanies this decision will become the guiding force for current and future generations - what one generation allows the next is forced to live with and endure.

As a result, the nation of Israel was split into two kingdoms, and a man named Jeroboam was thrust into a place and a position that should not have been given him. Jeroboam, because of fear of losing his authority, chose to establish idolatry and the worship of images made by hand (1 Kings 12:25-35). It is interesting to consider his reasoning and then to consider the lasting impact his decision would have.

Jeroboam said in his heart, "Now the kingdom will return to the house of David. If this people go up to offer sacrifices in the house of the LORD at Jerusalem, then the heart of this people will return to their lord, even to Rehoboam king of Judah; and

they will kill me and return to Rehoboam king of Judah."
1 Kings 12:26-27

As a nation, Israel was involved in a continual turning away from God and His ways, with a history of instant gratification and living in the moment. It seemed that any time God did not act or do things in the manner and at the time they desired, the people would quickly turn to idolatry or religion. A society or community driven by results will quickly downplay or forsake any semblance of relationship in order to get the outcome or results they desire. From the beginning, God was seeking to establish a relationship with man. Out of that relationship, God had promised blessings (results) that would far surpass anything man had seen or could imagine. Yet, these very people were continually forsaking God's plan to find a new way to satisfy their lust and desire.

God's manner is best summed up in the following manner: He desires to establish and maintain relationship with man. Out of the relationship with man, the proper roles designed to represent that relationship are established and understood. When each party understands their roles within the context of the relationship, they become aware of their responsibilities. Out of this healthy model the results will take care of themselves. The problem, however, is that when results are the focus this entire model is turned backwards and the relationship that should drive the vehicle is often left out entirely.

God's Prophetic Response

Jeroboam dishonored God, and he led God's people away from Him. How did God respond? God responded by establishing a prophetic destiny without immediately impacting reality. Jeroboam did experience a physical response to

God's presence, and there was destruction to the pagan altars; but, we still find that idolatry and opposition to God's established plan continued to weave its way through the history of Israel (1 Kings 13:4-5). While God had set in the spirit what would one day manifest in the natural, He was also permitting His people to live with the natural choices they had made. How often do people assume or even expect that no matter how foolish we behave, God is simply going to fix everything with only minor consequence?

God spoke destiny that would be realized three-hundred years later. Yet, at just the right time and in just the right way, God brought revival and restoration to His people.

Now behold, there came a man of God from Judah to Bethel by the word of the LORD, while Jeroboam was standing by the altar to burn incense. He cried against the altar by the word of the LORD, and said, "O altar, altar, thus says the LORD, 'Behold, a son shall be born to the house of David, Josiah by name; and on you he shall sacrifice the priests of the high places who burn incense on you, and human bones shall be burned on you.'" Then he gave a sign the same day, saying, "This is the sign which the LORD has spoken, 'Behold, the altar shall be split apart and the ashes which are on it shall be poured out.'" 1 Kings 13:1-3

God prophetically declared that He would bring things to order by re-establishing the reign of David, through a future king named Josiah. By definition, Josiah means "whom Jehovah heals." The implied destiny is that through King Josiah, God would heal the land and restore His place and His people. God was promising to bring revival to the land, declaring that through the life of Josiah He would bring His presence and His fire that would purge and heal the land.

Although it would be three-hundred years before Josiah was born, he was given the destiny of carrying a torch for revival.

Even before this prophetic declaration was made, God had already established His plan for healing the land. When Solomon, the son of David, was dedicating the temple he declared,

And My people who are called by My name humble themselves and pray and seek My face and turn from their wicked ways, then I will hear from heaven, will forgive their sin and will heal their land. 2 Chronicles 7:14

This verse has been quoted many times, in many places, and by many people. It is a wonderful promise from God. The prophetic declaration given about Josiah shortly after the death of Solomon is a further reminder of this promise from God. Josiah was a king definitely and specifically called by name. Josiah was a king who sought God's face and prayed for His direction and favor. Josiah, a man whose very name speaks of God healing, saw a great healing of the land take place in his day. Whenever God sets destiny in motion, He does so completely. We will further develop how Josiah fulfilled this prayer and the prophetic declaration about himself in Chapter Four.

Man seems naturally programmed to expect a response or reaction to every occurrence. Since it is often true that as humans we can rarely let things go by without doing something, we naturally assume God is the same. At some point it is as if we have determined God is created in our image.

When Jeroboam turned the people away from worship of The God of Israel, the established atmosphere was pregnant with possibilities for a move of God. There must have been many who were awaiting something drastic and supernatural from God. While we are implored to expect and anticipate great things from God, we must balance that with a willingness to trust God in whatever it is that He chooses to do. Situations and circumstances may not always line up with our preference, but God is always trustworthy. We are called by God to trust Him with all of our heart. While our mind may not be able to grasp what is taking place; in our hearts, where Christ dwells, we can have the peace and assurance that God is truly in control.

God is truly a God of order; He controls and directs all things. Throughout the Bible we find that He is always timely and specific in His actions. While it might be easy to assume that in this situation or in others like it, God is going to immediately act and prove Himself - that is not necessarily the case. While it might be easy to assume that when God does not immediately react it somehow makes Him weak or careless - that is definitely not the case. There is such a difference between reaction and response. It is of natural order and even physics to react; every action is met by an equal and opposite reaction. It is automatic, but a response is not automatic. It is what is best in light of the big picture. A reaction is in the moment, a response is with a longer term perspective.

Whereas a reaction may seem appropriate and even beneficial in the moment, the lasting consequences can sometimes undo any immediately realized good. Perspective need not be limited to the moment at hand. While we are able to view our segment of the puzzle, God has the entire finished product in clear view, and He will not get ahead of Himself.

When the Time Was Right

God's plan and destiny for the life of the one reading this book has been established in the spirit. There is a day coming where each individual will realize his purpose and know that for such a time as this God has brought him forth. For those who, like Josiah, carry the torch for revival, it is imperative to allow that torch to blaze inside your heart, so that when the time is right that fire will come forth from within and ignite a blazing fire in the place in which you find yourself. When Sumrall, Ratliff, and Cho gave their prophetic words about the revival in Pensacola, there was no way of knowing when that destiny would be realized. But God is faithful and will not allow His word to return unto Him void (Isaiah 55).

When I gave my life to Christ it was during a time of revival that was taking place at a church in my hometown. I remember watching family and friends get excited about God and His Spirit. It was both frustrating and enticing to me. The night God changed my life I actually remember making an appearance at church to try and convince myself and others that I was doing alright spiritually. God had other plans, and I had an encounter with His fire and presence. I can still hear the Evangelist singing the Karen Wheaton song *"Fire Shut Up in My Bones"* as I was making my way to the altar. I could literally feel a burning from within me. I was eighteen years old, and I was just beginning to step into my own destiny. God had placed a fire inside of me while in my mother's womb and on that June night in Indiana, God was causing me to sense true purpose for the first time in my life.

What I learned was the same thing Josiah and those around him learned. It is supernatural when destiny overtakes reality. The beauty about destiny is that it can overtake reality at any point. Destiny is not biased toward gender, toward social status, toward economic status, or toward age. Josiah was only eight years old when he became king. He then found himself in a position for the realization of his destiny. Destiny is not a destination; rather it is a journey. Josiah did not fulfill his prophetic destiny by simply becoming king. As the story unfolds we realize that it was at the age of twenty when he truly began to fulfill God's purpose. Some very important and significant things took place in the life of Josiah from the age of eight to twenty, and it was not just physical development.

So many people want to immediately step into all that God has for them. But, at eight, Josiah was not prepared to do what God would have him to do at twenty. God's preparation is critical. Otherwise, when destiny becomes reality it can overwhelm both the individual and those around them. As I sit here writing this book, I am reminded that my salvation story I shared above took place over sixteen years ago. I cannot begin to tell you all that God has shown me, taught me, and allowed me to experience in that time.

The torch for revival that God placed in my heart while I was in my mother's womb was ignited at salvation, and in the years since has led me to many fascinating places. Within six months of accepting Christ, I found myself in the midst of a multi-week revival as I was attending college. It was during this time that I was baptized in water and accepted the call of God to preach. I can still picture myself standing in front of another minster asking him to pray for me. As he was about to pray he asked me what I was going to do with the rest of my life. I turned the knob and opened the doorway to my destiny as I publicly declared for the first time that I was going to be a preacher. I still remember feeling like those words burst out of me before I even had time to develop the thought. God was aligning things in my life that would put me on the path toward fulfilling my destiny.

Growing in God

Josiah was eight years old when he became king.

Yes, Josiah had the title of king, and he was recognized by those around him as being king. At the age of eight, however, he did not yet have the capacity to be king. Josiah did not fully fulfill his destiny simply by sitting on the throne; that was simply the beginning of the fulfillment. It was necessary for Josiah to grow and learn within the context of being king. In Chapter Three we will explore the ways in which, even as a young child, King Josiah did what was right in the eyes of the Lord and followed the ways of his father David.

So often we wrongfully assume we have arrived, but in reality what we call the place of arrival God calls the place of beginning. Consider the Disciples of Christ for a moment. What did Jesus say to Simon and Andrew as they were fishing?

And Jesus said to them, "Follow Me, and I will make you become fishers of men." Mark 1:17

It would be wrong for us to assume that the moment they left their nets and followed Jesus their destiny was complete. At that moment, they were stepping through the doorway of destiny, and inside that place is where they would begin to learn and understand what it meant to become something different than what they were.

I can remember a time when my dad was taking us on vacation, and the trip was only about three hours away; although with my dad it could turn into four or five hours. Dad had promised so many fun things awaiting us at our destination. The days leading up to the trip were filled with anticipation of what we would do and how much fun we would have. Yet, as the drive seemed endless, the complaints grew louder. Finally, my dad took an exit off the interstate. I assumed it was to get gas or that he perhaps knew a better route, but actually he had heard enough, and we were not going to make it to our destination. We spent one night in some run down hotel with nothing to do and then we went back home. As a young boy, I did not believe that getting there was half the fun. Because I wanted to arrive without the drive, I missed out on what had been promised.

Peter did not step away from the fishing shores and into the Day of Pentecost. It would have been much easier, but would the catch have been as large? Along the journey toward destiny there were things Peter had to learn and have developed in his life. He had to learn how to become a fisher of men. We could consider many biblical stories that align with this very important principle. Joseph went through the process of becoming from the time of his dream until the time of the reality of that dream. Jesus Himself spent thirty years in preparation for three years of ministry. Is it not ironic that today we expect thirty years of effective ministry from three years of preparation? Many want power, prestige, and position without preparation.

There is something very important for us to understand before we leave this chapter. When you carry the torch for revival and your destiny overtakes reality do not miss that within that context God desires you to become prepared for your destiny. My heart breaks when I consider the history of revival and how so many revivals ceased because those entrusted with what God was doing were not willing to become what He was trying to make of them. Josiah was thrust into a powerful place at the age of eight. He was stepping into his destiny. As you read the story, however, you quickly realize that he never made it about himself. He always knew and understood that what God was doing was so much bigger than he or anyone else. He understood that he had a responsibility to become what God needed and desired him to be. Imagine the story if Josiah never progressed past where he was mentally, emotionally, physically, or spiritually at the age of eight. How might history look as a result?

Once during a time of prayer about what God was doing in my own life and ministry, I began to sense some powerful truths that the Lord wanted me to understand. I was trying to figure out why on the surface it seemed God was not doing as much as He had been doing recently. I'm not saying the lights had gone out, but it seemed they had dimmed. I asked the Lord for clarification, and what He shared with me I want to pass on to you.

Revival or a move of God is typically accompanied or recognized by moments of refreshing or what I call *pops* from God. The sense of His presence is beyond description, and there are various reactions and manifestations that take place in response to God's presence. A renewed sense of God's nearness and power can become overwhelming. I seriously doubt that anyone reading this enjoys God's pops any more than me. I love God's presence, His nearness, and seeing people encounter Him in a real and personal way. What happens, however, between the pops? This is something that

I have struggled with for years. So many times I have wondered why we could not live on the pops all the time.

Between the pops is where something very important takes place. It is called *growth.* When God, by His spirit and power, pops in your life and propels you forward into a new place in Him, there is a gap that is established, but nobody wants to talk about the gap. Everyone wants to talk about the new place you are in Christ and the joy found therein. Yet, from even a natural perspective any kind of a gap has to be filled. When a person experiences a pop to a new place in the Lord, if that gap is not filled and developed with growth, that person will reconnect with what he has always known or been comfortable with and he will revert back to where he was before and the pop will have been for naught. Here is how Jesus explains it:

"Now when the unclean spirit goes out of a man, it passes through waterless places seeking rest, and does not find it. Then it says, 'I will return to my house from which I came'; and when it comes, it finds it unoccupied, swept, and put in order. Then it goes and takes along with it seven other spirits more wicked than itself, and they go in and live there; and the last state of that man becomes worse than the first. That is the way it will also be with this evil generation." Matthew 12:43-45

If Josiah had everything he needed at age eight to do what God had called him to do, his destiny would have been realized then and not twelve years later. Josiah experienced a *pop* from God when he was placed on the throne. But the success of his reign was that he became king through *growth*.

There is always more that God wants to teach us and cause us to become. Our destiny is not realized by the pops; our destiny is sustained in the growth. If a person pops from point A to point B and does not fill the gap with growth where will they find themselves when the next pop happens? On the other hand, when growth fills the gap, the next pop is not a repeat of going from point A to point B. Rather, the next pop is from point B to point C. The pops are necessary to take us to new levels and places in Him. But if we do not have the growth in place to become then what we have is merely a shallow experience.

Chapter 2 – Sustaining the Reign

Josiah was eight years old when he became king, and he reigned thirty-one years in Jerusalem. He did right in the sight of the LORD, and walked in the ways of his father David and did not turn aside to the right or to the left. 2 Chronicles 34:1-2

Reign with Him

Josiah was eight years old when he became king, and he reigned . . .

To reign means to possess or exercise sovereign power or authority; to have control, rule, or influence of any kind. As king, Josiah was given authority, control, and influence over the dealings of those under his rule. Josiah was given a high position – a position of authority. The destiny that he was stepping into was not only employing; it was also empowering. Anytime that God brings a person into a place of destiny He empowers them to succeed. Where God guides He provides; what God ordains He sustains.

God's design is to bring us into our destiny with Him and empower us to reign. One of the biggest mistakes we often make as Christians is forgetting who we are in Christ. Peter declares about the people of God,

But you are a chosen race, a royal priesthood, a holy nation, a people for God's own possession, so that you may proclaim the excellencies of Him who has called you out of darkness into His marvelous light. 1 Peter 2:9

Note the descriptive words about believers. We are chosen, we are royalty, we are holy, and we are God's special possession. But how often do we live far below where God intends? How often do we settle for less than what God has for us?

One of my least favorite things to hear is for someone to speak about being under the circumstances. Ask someone how they are doing and you may hear, "Under the circumstances I am doing fine." Friends, we are not called to be under anything. Consider these statements of truth:

The LORD will make you the head and not the tail, and you only will be above, and you will not be underneath, if you listen to the commandments of the LORD your God, which I charge you today, to observe them carefully, Deuteronomy 28:13

Who will separate us from the love of Christ? Will tribulation, or distress, or persecution, or famine, or nakedness, or peril, or sword? Just as it is written, "For your sake we are being put to death all day long; we were considered as sheep to be slaughtered." But in all these things we overwhelmingly conquer through Him who loved us. For I am convinced that neither death, nor life, nor angels, nor principalities, nor things present, nor things to come, nor powers, nor height, nor depth, nor any other created thing, will be able to separate us from the love of God, which is in Christ Jesus our Lord. Romans 8:35-39

You are from God, little children, and have overcome them; because greater is He who is in you than he who is in the world. 1 John 4:4

These will wage war against the Lamb, and the Lamb will overcome them, because He is Lord of lords and King of kings, and those who are with Him are the called and chosen and faithful." Revelation 17:14

Are you getting this? God has made you the head and not the tail. God has placed you at the top and not the bottom. Nothing shall separate us from the love of God that is in Christ. Greater is the One in you than the one in the world. God speaks very highly of His people. As the King of kings, He is the Royalty over royalty. And since He reigns over all, we cannot forget that He has created us to reign with Him. When God created man, His declaration was for man to "have dominion" (Genesis 1:26). From the beginning, God's design has been for man to reign. The Psalmist declared:

When I consider Your heavens, the work of Your fingers, the moon and the stars, which You have ordained; what is man that You take thought of him, and the son of man that You care for him? Yet You have made him a little lower than God, and You crown him with glory and majesty! You make him to rule over the works of Your hands; You have put all things under his feet, Psalm 8:3-6

Revival is the process of restoring God's people back to the place He designed for them. Revival aligns us with God's purpose, it brings about life and church done in God's way, and it places us into Kingdom authority as God desires. Revival causes God's people to reign in the manner in which He intended.

We get ourselves into so much trouble by viewing God and our position in Him through the eyes of our circumstances. That is never a view of victory. At no point do I picture King Josiah fretting over the circumstances around him to the point that he did nothing in response. Rather, I picture him viewing each situation with the understanding that he was king and was able to rule and reign over any and all circumstances. Plus, I do not imagine he needed people to constantly remind him he was king. Josiah lived with the conviction and assurance that he was royalty. Out of that position, he did what was right.

I cannot tell you how many times I have prayed that God would cause all of us to understand who we are in Him. Like Josiah, we are royalty. As such, we can rule and reign. We can live victoriously. We need revival so that we can "be transformed by the renewing of our minds" (Romans 12:2). We must change our way of thinking so that we can grasp this truth of living victoriously. The natural tendency of our minds and our actions is to think and act contrary to God's intent. As believers, we have the "mind of Christ" (1 Corinthians 2:16); let us therefore be led by His thoughts and desires and not our own. Once we win the battle in our mind we will win the battle in our world, and begin to reign as God intends.

Reign Over Circumstance

There is no reason for us to bow to circumstances or situations in our lives or in our world. We must only bow our knee to God. There is no way for us to avoid difficulties in life. Life has a way of presenting challenges. As the people of God *we do not belong to those who shrink back and are destroyed, but to those who have faith and are saved (Hebrews 10:39).* The reality is that as Christians we are not exempt from battles, challenges and difficulties. But, the beauty is that because of the work of God's Spirit in our hearts and lives, we can and will be victorious. God desires us to reign over our circumstances. I love the way the prophet Isaiah described it.

But now, thus says the LORD, your Creator, O Jacob, and He who formed you, O Israel, "Do not fear, for I have redeemed you; I have called you by name; you are Mine! "When you pass through the waters, I will be with you; and through the rivers, they will not overflow you. When you walk through the fire, you will not be scorched, nor will the flame burn you. "For I am the LORD your God, the Holy One of Israel, your Savior; Isaiah 43:1-3

God's promise is not that we will avoid the waters, rivers or even the fire. His promise is that we will pass through them. We allow circumstances to reign over us when we do not proceed, but instead allow these things to stop us. From our perspective it may look impassable or impossible; however, God will be with us and will see us through the challenges. When revival breaks out in our heart and life, we come to the place that we see circumstances as another opportunity for God to reveal Himself and show Himself strong. Life is not about what happens to us, but rather life is about how we respond to what happens to us.

Reign Over Sin

Paul instructs the Romans:

For you have not received a spirit of slavery leading to fear again, but you have received a spirit of adoption as sons by which we cry out, "Abba! Father!" Romans 8:15

Revival restores purity and victory over sin. Rules without relationship lead to rebellion. The problem is that for so long in the church we have tried to go against this idea. I will tread lightly, but legalistic tendencies that have infiltrated the life of the church have pushed away more than they have drawn. At the same time, the anything goes, liberalism mentality that has infiltrated the church has been just as damaging.

In both situations the impetus is on the believers to determine the right way to serve God. This goes against God's design. Revival positions you in a place to reign over sin, because it puts the focus on the relationship with God. Just as we are human *beings* and not human *doings*, so are we to *be* Christians and not try so hard to *do* Christianity. We can never effectively *do* what God has called us to *be*.

When God's Spirit comes alive in your heart, out of that relationship will come a desire to please Him. The most lasting and effective relationships operate in this manner. I am not married to my wife because she makes me happy – although she does. My ultimate purpose in our marriage is to make her happy. I do not want to hurt or damage her; I love her. I do not spend my time thinking about what I do not get to do because I am married. Rather, I relish all the blessings, beauties, and benefits of the relationship I enjoy with my wife.

The same can and should be said for our relationship with God. There are so many wonderful things that God has called us to do that there is simply no reason to focus on the do not's. I do not spend my time thinking about how I wish I could steal. I do not spend my time disappointed that I cannot go out and kill someone. Rather, I relish all the blessings, beauties, and benefits of the relationship I enjoy with God through Christ.

In David's prayer of repentance he declares that he was "shapen in iniquity" (Psalm 51:5). Iniquity is the crooked or bent nature within each of us. Our flesh operates from that crooked place and will constantly sin or miss the mark. Iniquity, if not kept in check, can become the force that drives our lives. Iniquity and sin gain authority when we become lax in our relationship with God. Look again at the verse from Romans,

For you have not received a spirit of slavery leading to fear again, but you have received a spirit of adoption as sons by which we cry out, "Abba! Father!" Romans 8:15

The victory described here is that which is established in relationship. We are God's children; He is our Father. When revival brings this relationship back into focus and at the forefront, we find ourselves victorious over sin.

Reign Over Poverty

As God's children, we are also recipients of His blessings. Revival and the move of His Spirit cause us to reign over poverty. I am not simply referring to poverty from a financial standpoint, but more so the spirit of poverty. As I stated earlier, there are far too many Christians and far too many churches that settle for less than what God has for them. The primary reason is often a spirit of poverty. This is a feeling that what we have is all we deserve and we can never do or have better. I echo the sentiments of John in his letter,

Beloved, I pray that in all respects you may prosper and be in good health, just as your soul prospers. 3 John 1:2

Christians should be the best and most successful people in the world. I cannot find any reason for believers to just get by socially, economically, physically, or in any other way. God's plan and desire is for you to succeed. God's desire is for you to walk in *abundant life (John 10:10)*. So many get concerned and uncomfortable about money and the dangers it can bring. The issue here is the same as what we discussed above in reigning over sin: when the relationship

31

with God is the focus, you will walk in victory. If we lose focus and turn to money or things as our provision, then the issues will arise. I once heard Tommy Tenney say, "When you learn how to handle the glory, everything you touch will turn to gold." Revival and the move of God's Spirit in and through your life will bring you to a place of blessing and prosperity in all things.

In Chapter Four we will dive further into the importance of seeking God and not revival. It is imperative that we do not go after God for what He can do, but rather we hunger for God because of Who He is. God's blessings are a by-product of the relationship, not the point of the relationship. God's desire and design is that we reign.

And raised us up with Him, and seated us with Him in the heavenly places in Christ Jesus, so that in the ages to come He might show the surpassing riches of His grace in kindness toward us in Christ Jesus. Ephesians 2:6-7

Reign in the City

Josiah was eight years old when he became king, and he reigned thirty-one years in Jerusalem.

Revival is not just about *how* you reign; it is about *where* you reign as well. Josiah took over for some sinful predecessors, and Jerusalem was ripe for revival. Consider the following excerpt from *Charisma Reports: The Brownsville Revival* by Marcia Ford. In speaking about the prophetic word given by Dr. Cho, she writes,

His finger rested on Pensacola, a Florida panhandle city hardly associated with spiritual fervor. In fact, the city was known to the homosexual community as the "gay Riviera." A seven-mile stretch of beach on the Gulf of Mexico just east of

*the city attracted thousands of homosexuals and lesbians;
over the Memorial Day weekend every year, the homosexual
population reached as high as fifty thousand. Pensacola was
definitely one place to be if you were gay.*

*It was also the place to be if you wanted an abortion. At one
time, the city was home to three abortion clinics. Three clinic
bombings on Christmas Eve of 1984 had put Pensacola on
the map; within three years of Cho's vision, the murders of
three clinic workers had drawn worldwide attention to the city
of fifty-eight thousand people.*

Just as Jerusalem was ripe for a move of God prior to the reign of Josiah, so was Pensacola prior to the Brownsville Revival. Yes, God wants individuals to experience revival. Yes, God wants churches to experience revival. Ultimately, however, God desires His Kingdom to reign in cities and regions. God's ways and thoughts are higher than ours (Isaiah 55); let us not think, dream, or act in small ways. Where are you right now geographically? God wants to reign in your city; God wants to reign in your region. Consider this:

*But indeed, as I live, all the earth will be filled with the glory of
the LORD. Numbers 14:21*

*They will not hurt or destroy in all My holy mountain, for
the earth will be full of the knowledge of the LORD as the
waters cover the sea. Isaiah 11:9*

*"For the earth will be filled with the knowledge of the glory of
the LORD, as the waters cover the sea. " Habakkuk 2:14*

Matthew 18:16 declares that words are established from the mouth of two or three witnesses. By the mouth of Moses, Isaiah, and Habakkuk, God declared that the earth

33

would be filled with His glory and the knowledge of His glory. God is serious about this. Seeing as He has declared this destiny, it is only a matter of time until it becomes a reality. God's glory will cover the earth, and *in order for God's glory to cover the earth it has to start somewhere.*

How about Billings, Montana? Perhaps the glory cover could start in Sacramento, California. Why not Landover, Maryland? What a wonderful thing it would be for God to break out in Washington, D.C. Or, maybe God's ignition is your hometown or current place of residence. God has planted you right where you are on purpose and with a purpose. That purpose is for His Spirit to be poured out upon your life, enabling His Kingdom to reign in you and through you to your city.

In the early 1800s, God was using Charles Finney in a powerful way. What strikes me in reading stories from those days is the number of towns and cities that were experiencing revival. People were being converted in workplaces, schoolhouses, inns, and on the streets - not just in churches. God was after cities and in Finney he found someone through whom He would reach those cities. Wesley Duewel wrote a book entitled *Revival Fire* in which he recounts stories and experiences from some great historical moves of God. I was struck by this paragraph.

Finney lists the "striking characteristics" of these revivals as 1. The prevalence of a mighty Spirit of prevailing prayer. 2. Overwhelming conviction of sin. 3. Sudden and powerful conversions to Christ. 4. Great love and abounding joy of the converts. 5. Intelligence and stability of the converts. 6. Their great earnestness, activity, and usefulness in the prayers and labors for others. (Duewel, 1995, p. 105).

The true impact of God's presence cannot be contained within the walls of any church building. God wants to reign in cities. May we allow God by His Spirit and power to flow in and through our lives, to see His Kingdom come and His will be done in our part of the earth as it is in Heaven.

Sustaining the Reign

Josiah was eight years old when he became king, and he reigned thirty-one years in Jerusalem.

At the close of Chapter One we examined the value and importance of combining the pops of God with the time of growth. God intends for what He does in our lives to be sustained and to continue long term. A quick search of the list of the kings who reigned in either the northern or southern kingdom will find varying lengths of those reigns. The range is from seven days to fifty-five years. Josiah's reign was for thirty-one years. How was he able to reign so long? How was Josiah able to sustain what God was doing? What can we learn and apply within our own context of revival? I want to explore five key components for sustaining revival.

Leadership

It is imperative that the leaders of a move of God live, act, and rule with confidence and consistency. During the thirty-one year reign of Josiah there was never a question about his style or approach as king. Imagine how quickly he would have lost his authority had he been inconsistent. People are looking for a leader who knows where he is going.

Confidence and consistency must be shown in how you respond to and handle what God is doing. I have been in revival services where the leader would declare, "I have no idea what is going on or what we should do." While it may have seemed he was trusting God and being spontaneous, for those in the service it did not give a feeling of security. If the leader(s) did not know what was happening, then who did? If you are leading a revival, I do not mean that you have to control what is going on or totally understand what is going on – but the people under your leadership deserve a leader who leads with confidence and consistency.

I am not implying that we must have all the answers; only God fits the bill of omniscience. Yet, learning to lead within the context of what God is doing is vitally important for maintaining the move of God.

Exaltation of God

Worship is critical in sustaining what God is doing. As God is honored in worship, His presence will continue. The Psalmist teaches us that God dwells where praises are offered to Him.

But You are holy, O You Who dwell in [the holy place where] the praises of Israel [are offered]. Psalm 22:3 (Amplified)

God dwells where praises are offered. This speaks of sustained revival. When I speak of revival I am not referring to a visitation from God; rather, I speak of a habitation or dwelling of God's presence. God's desire is to dwell among His people.

Let them construct a sanctuary for Me, that I may dwell among them. Exodus 25:8

I will dwell among the sons of Israel and will be their God. They shall know that I am the LORD their God who

brought them out of the land of Egypt, that I might dwell
among them; I am the LORD *their God.   Exodus 29:45-46*

"Concerning this house which you are building, if you will walk
in My statutes and execute My ordinances and keep all My
commandments by walking in them, then I will carry out My
word with you which I spoke to David your father. I will dwell
among the sons of Israel, and will not forsake My people
Israel." 1 Kings 6:12-13

If God desires to dwell among His people, and He dwells where praises are offered, by exalting and praising Him we can sustain His presence (revival). I continue to learn in my own life that the more I praise Him, the more of His presence I enjoy. Oftentimes the biggest challenge we face in terms of praise and worship is with the current circumstances of our life. Yet, we do not praise God for what He is doing, we praise God for Who He is. From this understanding is the only way that we can "rejoice in the Lord always" (Philippians 4:4). This approach allows us to give thanks "in everything" (1 Thessalonians 5:18).

I challenge each person reading this right now to lay this book aside and devote the next fifteen minutes to praising God. It does not matter if you cannot think of a reason to praise Him right now - praise Him because He is God. It does not matter if there are challenges in your life that make praise seem impossible. Praise Him because He is God. Praise God because praise brings His presence and in His presence is "fullness of joy" (Psalm 16:11). Praise and exaltation of God will sustain what He is doing.

Emphasis on Purity

God's desire is for His people to live right before Him. As discussed in Chapter One, I am not intending to see a shift back to human legalism. A look back to Deuteronomy, however, shows us God's plan from the beginning.

Behold, I set before you this day a blessing and a curse; A blessing, if ye obey the commandments of the LORD your God, which I command you this day: And a curse, if ye will not obey the commandments of the LORD your God, but turn aside out of the way which I command you this day, to go after other gods, which ye have not known. Deuteronomy 11:26-28

God's blessing is upon those who obey His commands and walk in purity. We quickly step outside of God's place of blessing when we turn away from His design. This is nothing new. We find this in the Garden of Eden where Adam and Eve lost God's blessing because of disobedience. Yes, they lost access to the Garden, but that was not the real issue. Up until that point, it was common for God to join Adam and Eve in the Garden. God would spend time with them and they would enjoy fellowship together. This was the true loss. Look at their response.

They heard the sound of the LORD God walking in the garden in the cool of the day, and the man and his wife hid themselves from the presence of the LORD God among the trees of the garden. Genesis 3:8

Because of their sin, they forfeited fellowship with God. Nothing will remove God's presence more quickly than sin. The way I see it the greatest form of judgment that God gives is the removal of His presence. I once heard my friend Joe Oden say, "The message of holiness might not be the recipe

38

to make friends, be popular, or build a mega church. It is however the recipe to see God." The modern anything goes religious ideology may not agree, but God's Word still does.

But your iniquities have made a separation between you and your God, And your sins have hidden His face from you so that He does not hear. Isaiah 59:2

In my own life as I have been in personal revival, I have made it a point to do what I can to sustain His presence. I have a part to play in maintaining His presence. I do not emphasize purity for the sake of religion. I want to please God, and maintain the purity of our relationship. The more importantly I view my relationship with God and His presence, the higher value I will place on personal purity.

Focus on God's Word

We can quickly undo what God is doing by getting away from His Word. Mark Twain once said, "*Most people are bothered by those passages of Scripture they do not understand, but the passages that bother me are those I do understand.*" God's Word is clear, precise and is the guiding force for His people. To sustain revival it is imperative that we keep His Word at the forefront.

During Josiah's reign, Hilkiah the priest found the Book of the Law (2 Chronicles 34:14). Josiah's response is a key factor in understanding how he was able to sustain his reign as king.

Then the king stood in his place and made a covenant before the LORD to walk after the LORD, and to keep His commandments and His testimonies and His statutes with all his heart and with all his soul, to perform the words of the covenant written in this book. 2 Chronicles 34:31

Josiah made a conscious choice and effort to focus on and follow God's Word. The result was that Josiah reigned thirty-one years and the people under his reign enjoyed a revival of God's presence and favor. In Chapter Nine we will dig further into how Josiah responded to God's Word.

There are many books that have been written. There are many opinions that have been shared. There are many seminars and conferences that have been held and attended. But God's Word stands alone as the only infallible source of truth and direction for life.

Trusting God

The final factor to sustaining a move of God is trust. Over the last several months of my life I have been learning the importance of trust. Some time ago I was going through a very difficult time in my life, especially with regards to ministry. I distinctly remember telling God and anyone who would listen that I was done preaching, pastoring, and being in ministry all together. I was dejected, discouraged, and disappointed. I was viewing things from the wrong perspective.

Pastor Richard Crisco once said, "Real Revelation does not come from questions we ask God but from questions He asks us!" I found out how true this is. Late one night I was in my living room praying. I remember sensing God's presence, and thoroughly enjoying the worship and prayer. Then God spoke this in my heart: "Can I ask you a question?" Of course I responded that He could ask me anything. You might want to think about that response; He will take you seriously. I thought I was ready for any question. But, God surprised me when He asked, "Do you trust Me?" Easy one, right? Actually it was not. I remember stopping dead in my tracks and taking a moment to ensure I heard Him right. I had. I knew in my mind and from what I had even preached and taught that the answer was obviously a resounding yes. In that moment, however, I could not answer.

God is more interested in sincerity from our hearts than rote answers from our minds.

I remember telling God, "I do not know." I told Him I knew I should trust Him but that I was not sure I could answer that question. I began to share with Him how I felt He had let me down and how I was afraid to trust Him. Amazingly enough He did not strike me dead on the spot. I say that somewhat tongue-in-cheek. In reality, so many are afraid to be honest with God. We would much rather give a trained response than to say what we really think or feel. Yet, God is more interested in sincerity from our hearts than rote answers from our minds.

This conversation about trust went on for at least three days – although it seemed much longer at the time. I can still see myself lying in bed the night I answered this question from my heart. I simply said, "Yes, Lord, I trust You." He simply replied, "Ok." While I expected something supernatural and amazing to happen in that moment it did not. From that moment, however, God has amazed me again and again as I continue to learn to trust in Him. The key is to:

Trust in the LORD *with all your heart and do not lean on your own understanding. In all your ways acknowledge Him, And He will make your paths straight. Proverb 3:5-6*

God's call to me and to all of us is for a trust that comes from our hearts. There are times that things simply do not line up with our minds or from our perspective. In those moments, trust seems impossible. But, God is always trustworthy. Learning to trust God will take you to, and keep you in, new places in Him.

When God begins to move we want to sustain His presence. Through Godly leadership, exalting God, maintaining purity, focusing on God's Word, and trusting Him we can sustain His presence. Revival is God's ways in action. It is not God's intention to see things revert back to our own ways. Let us press in and press on to sustain revival. As we do our part, God's Spirit can and will reign.

Our Role in Revival

He did right in the sight of the LORD, and walked in the ways of his father David and did not turn aside to the right or to the left.

So what must we do? What can we do? Yes, God in His sovereignty can do whatever He chooses with or without our involvement. Yet, we find throughout His Word and throughout history that He chooses to use and partner with man.

Dwight L. Moody heard his friend Henry Varley say, *"The world has yet to see what God can do with and for and through and in a man who is fully and wholly consecrated to Him."* Moody was so moved by this statement that he dedicated his life to becoming that man. Are there others like Moody who will choose to partner with God and make a difference?

The most important thing that God is looking for is not your ability – it is your availability. What God has placed inside of you is exactly what He needs to make a difference through you. Do not allow what God has placed in your life to lay dormant and unused.

For I am mindful of the sincere faith within you, which first dwelt in your grandmother Lois and your mother Eunice, and I am sure that it is in you as well. For this reason I remind you to kindle afresh the gift of God which is in you through the laying on of my hands. For God has not given us a spirit of timidity, but of power and love and discipline.
2 Timothy 1:5-7

In December 2011, our church hosted a friend who is both an evangelist and a revivalist. During one of the services he asked if he could pray for me. As he began to pray, he asked the Lord to stir up the gift that was in me. He prayed that God would bring out what He had placed in my life. I remember standing there feeling hands on my waist and stomach moving me around and pulling on me. I wanted to turn around and tell the person to let go so I could focus on what God was saying and doing. In my mind I was trying to determine who in our church had hands that strong. I later asked the evangelist and others who it was that was holding me by my waist. Each assured me that there was no human touching or holding onto me. In that moment, God was answering the prayer and was stirring up the gift He had already deposited.

From that moment, God has done things in and through me that have been at times overwhelming. Yet, I know that this is just the beginning. God desires to cover the earth with His glory and presence. And He is looking for willing individuals to make themselves available to Him. To close Chapter Two, let us consider one more verse of scripture. As you read this verse ask yourself if you are willing to be the fulfillment.

For the eyes of the LORD move to and fro throughout the earth that He may strongly support those whose heart is completely His. 2 Chronicles 16:9

Chapter 3 – Walking Right Before the Lord

He did right in the sight of the LORD, and walked in the ways of his father David and did not turn aside to the right or to the left.
2 Chronicles 34:2

Do What is Right

Many view the term Christian as a noun to describe them. The word Christian, however, is as much a verb as it is a noun. Christianity is active; Christianity is a mobile partnering with God to accomplish much for His Kingdom. If you are going to fulfill God's plan for your life, it is imperative that you actively participate in life as a Christian. But it is not enough to just act or be active. What we must do is act *righteously*. We are called to do what is right in the eyes of the Lord.

Consider how Josiah did what was right: he stayed focused and on course. He did not turn to the left or the right. He sought God even from an early age. He turned to God as his source of strength and direction. He purged Israel of sin, dealing aggressively with the sin in his land. He took responsibility for the entire kingdom and set things right. He had God's house repaired. He placed a high priority on God's Word. He was willing to repent personally and vicariously for the entire nation. Josiah gives us an ideal image of what it means to do what is right. In coming chapters we will take the time to consider these actions in more detail.

Productive Living

Jesus taught a valuable lesson in John 15 when He was speaking about Himself as the vine and us as the branches. An important truth is nestled into this passage:

You did not choose Me but I chose you, and appointed you that you would go and bear fruit, and that your fruit would remain, so that whatever you ask of the Father in My name He may give to you. John 15:16

Out of our relationship with Him, God desires that we produce fruit that will last. Christianity is not a destination, but rather a journey. When we accept Christ we begin the relationship with Him. His call is for us to produce fruit that keeps with or is worthy of our repentance (Matthew 3:8). The Amplified Bible adds, "Let your lives prove your change of heart." The fruit of righteousness, or doing what is right in the eyes of the Lord, should be the primary product of revival. Drawing on the image of becoming from Chapter One, consider what Paul says to the church in Corinth:

He made Him who knew no sin to be sin on our behalf, so that we might become the righteousness of God in Him.
2 Corinthians 5:21

Producing fruit does not happen immediately in any context. Yet as believers, out of the cultivated relationship with Christ we should become fruit producers. Love, joy, peace, forbearance,   kindness,   goodness,   faithfulness, gentleness and self-control (Galatians 5:22-23) should be evident in our lives and they should be lasting. What God does inside our hearts and inside our churches should be evident outside in our lives and daily walk. This correlates to the growth that must accompany the pops. An invaluable result of revival is allowing what God does *in us* to be done *through us*, which we discussed in Chapter One.

The balance is that, yes, we are saved by grace through faith (Ephesians 2:8-9); but our faith without works is dead (James 2). Actions truly do speak louder than words.

The value that we place on our relationship with God and what He is doing in our lives is going to be evident by what we do. Are we doing "what is right?" It is apparent that in life a person is either going to be a product of their life or they are going to be productive in life. I want my life to be both a representation of and a reflection of what God has done in and for me.

In terms of the concept of faith being dead without works, it is important to realize that our outward expressions, works, will flow naturally from our inward relationship with Christ. We cannot work enough to develop or establish ourselves in Christ, but what we do for Him flows out of the relationship that we have with and through Him.

When I consider my own course as a believer, I am overwhelmed with the influence that revival and God's manifest presence has had on my life. When I gave my life to Christ, it was during a revival in my home town. If I remember correctly I was the thirty-ninth person saved. About six months later, I was blessed to be a part of a revival in the city where I was attending college. During one of those services I came to full realization of God's call on my life to preach. About six months later, I found myself enrolled at Brownsville Revival School of Ministry, where for the next two years I was impacted with God's presence and fire in preparation for the fulfillment of God's call on my life. That personal heritage has sparked in me the drive and desire to do what is right. I want to produce fruit that is both worthy of the repentance I have been given as well as fruit that lasts. I want my walk with Christ to be a clear reflection of the great things He has done in my life. That is what revival produces. I want to be a living testimony of the power of revival.

In God's Eyes

But, you may ask, why is this so important? The answer: God is watching. Josiah did what was right "in the eyes of the Lord." That is the key. We do not choose to live right for the approval of man. If we do, our impure motives undo our pure actions. We have one Lord and Savior whose approval we should value above all.

Every Friday night during the Brownsville Revival a baptismal service took place. Each week we were able to hear testimonies of salvations and great things God was doing in the lives of individuals. On a number of occasions a pastor would step into the baptismal tank and share something like this, "I have been pastoring for twenty years but on Wednesday night I gave my life to Jesus Christ at these altars." These men and women had been actively involved in church ministry, yet something was missing. On the surface, they appeared to have it all together, yet their lives were lived for the eyes of man and not the eyes of God. Josiah did not just do what was right; he did so in the eyes of the Lord.

Revival will bring out many gifted and charismatic individuals. Charisma is something that will bring you into some great places in life. It is only character, however, that will sustain or keep you in those places. So many moves of God have been aborted because the leadership lived as characters rather than as men of character. It is imperative that we do what is right in the eyes of the Lord, thus honoring Him. It cannot just be done in public; it must be at the center of who we are. God is more interested in your character than in your charisma. God is more interested in your character than in your comfort.

I clearly remember a sermon by Evangelist Steve Hill in which he was preaching along these lines of character and living right before the Lord. To illustrate his message, he was using a camera to take pictures at various times during the message. He would snap a picture and proclaim, "God saw what you just did." He continued to drive home the point that even when we think we are in private, and when we think nobody is watching – God always sees. The lights in the Brownsville sanctuary were turned out during parts of this message. Things were extremely dark in that large room. You could still hear Rev. Hill sharing and then suddenly you would see this brilliant flash as he took yet another picture. Even then, in the dark, God saw. At the conclusion of the sermon, Rev Hill dumped a bag full of film canisters to show all the images that had been taken of a person's life. The best part of that night was when we were reminded that Jesus came to expose and clear the film and to give us a fresh start.

That is the picture and the key. We must do what is right in the eyes of the Lord, because He is watching. There are things we do that may not seem to be a big deal, but they are developing our character, the person we are. Just like Josiah, we have the opportunity in our lives to begin to do what is right in the eyes of the Lord. Let us each allow God's presence and power to produce the fruit of righteousness in our lives.

At the end of Chapter Two, we considered 2 Chronicles 16:9 where God says His eyes are looking for someone to show Himself strong on their behalf. God is watching and looking for someone through whom to manifest Himself. I want His eyes to catch me and be pleased with how I live, think, speak, and act. I want Him to show Himself strong in and through my life. We need not seek for a reputation or recognition from man. I do not live my life for your approval. I do not make everyone happy and not everyone agrees with how I choose to live. Yet when I sense God's presence and nearness in my life, and as I watch Him do great things, I am reminded that doing what is right is worth it all.

Where Are You Going?

He did right in the sight of the LORD, and walked in the ways of his father David and did not turn aside to the right or to the left.
2 Chronicles 34:2

Doing what is right is much harder when you are not moving. Stagnation and immobility lead to decline, decay, and death. Josiah was effective in his reign because "he walked." He was actively involved in the revival that God brought to Jerusalem. He did not stand on the sidelines or sit on the bench. He jumped in with both feet and got busy being about the Father's business. The fruit of God's Spirit is produced through the lives of the active. Many wish for things from God, while others move forward and get things from God. Consider this Proverb:

The soul of the sluggard craves and gets nothing,
But the soul of the diligent is made fat.. Proverb 13:4

God is sovereign and all-powerful and is able to do whatever He chooses; He chooses to act through you and me. We have a part to play in revival. God wants to show Himself strong on your behalf, but if you are stagnant and idle it makes it difficult for Him to do so.

Faith, Forward, Freedom

Each of us is at a different place in our faith in God. Neither you nor I can change where we are in this moment. I cannot spend my time wishing I was further along in my faith. Where I am is where I am. I cannot change yesterday and I cannot predict tomorrow; but I can affect right now. The key is learning to find where you are now and viewing that as your starting point, understanding that faith is now. Take a good look at yourself and realistically assess where you are in your faith. There is no condemnation or judgment needed. All that matters is where you find yourself, because that is the perfect place to be right now.

Now that you realize where you stand, it is time to move. In terms of walking with God and living our faith there is only one direction we should be moving, and that direction is forward. We have no reason to retreat or stand still. Many of us can attest to the ineffectiveness of standing still. Therefore, our choice is forward. God is always calling us forward in our relationship with Him. This is growth and discipleship. This is our faith developing and allowing us to continue to do what is right in the eyes of the Lord.

The only time that you do not move forward is when you are settled into a comfort zone. I know from experience how easy it can be to let that happen. You find yourself in a place in God that is pleasant and appealing, and the easiest thing to do is to relax and become stagnant. As Jesus was transfigured before His disciples in Matthew 17 that was Peter's reaction: let's pitch a tent and stay here. But when we stay in one place we sacrifice God's best on the altar of His good; often giving up so much for so little.

But what happens when we do move forward with God and we come face to face with an obstacle that seems impossible? Think for a moment about the children of Israel and their exodus from Egypt. It took a great amount of faith

51

for them to pack up and leave what had been their home for generations. It took a great amount of faith for them to continue to journey in obedience to God. But imagine the horror they must have felt when they found themselves stuck between the Red Sea and the Egyptian army.

In considering this story, the Lord once asked me, "Do you think I was surprised to find the Red Sea in their way?" I had never thought of it in that way. God had been leading them the entire way and had simply asked them to follow Him. He could have chosen another route that did not encounter the sea. God knew full well that His people were going to come face to face with an immovable object. As God is leading us, He is not caught off guard when we encounter challenges or obstacles. He does not fumble through a playbook to find something else to do. He does not pull together a heavenly research team to redirect the path of His people. As God saw it the Red Sea was not an obstacle, it was part of the journey. Look what Exodus says:

The angel of God, who had been going before the camp of Israel, moved and went behind them; and the pillar of cloud moved from before them and stood behind them. So it came between the camp of Egypt and the camp of Israel; and there was the cloud along with the darkness, yet it gave light at night. Thus the one did not come near the other all night.
Exodus 14:19-20

The children of Israel were led by a pillar of cloud by day and a pillar of fire by night. When the pillar moved, they would follow. The pillar would always be in front leading them. Consider this image for a moment: the Israelites are standing before the Red Sea in fear as the Egyptians are closing in from behind them. The Angel of the Lord and the pillar moved behind them while they passed through the waters. That means the pillar of cloud was already crossing the Red Sea. This was the way God was going to take His people. The Red Sea was simply part of the journey. It was neither a stop sign nor a detour. As we move forward with God we cannot allow barriers or obstacles to stop or detour us. We should never call an obstacle what God says is an opportunity. We cannot be dictated by difficulty – but directed by Divinity.

Do you remember what Moses said to the people?

But Moses said to the people, "Do not fear! Stand by and see the salvation of the LORD which He will accomplish for you today; for the Egyptians whom you have seen today, you will never see them again forever. The LORD will fight for you while you keep silent." Exodus 14:13-14

To Moses this seemed like the right thing to say and do, but it upset God. God was not upset that Moses told the people that God would deliver them; God was upset because Moses told the people to stand still. They were only to stand still when the pillar was not moving. The cloud was still moving, so they should be moving too. Look at God's response:

Then the LORD said to Moses, "Why are you crying out to Me? Tell the sons of Israel to go forward." Exodus 14:15

To God, standing still was not an option. He said to go forward. The same is true for us. It does not matter if we find ourselves in a place that is comfortable or a place that is perilous; the only direction to go from that place is forward. It was only after the people stopped and Moses made his declaration that we find the pillar moved from the front to the back of the people. Their stopping was their own choice and not God's directing.

It was almost as if God was moving behind them to compel or push them forward, because they obviously were not responding to His leading in the proper manner this time. This is the only time we read about the children of Israel moving without the pillar in front of them. God's direction is always forward. And in those times when we do not follow His leading from in front of us, He may very well move behind to compel us forward. Those steps of faith can be even more treacherous or uncertain. The best response from us is to always move forward with God leading from the front.

The result of starting from where you are in your faith and moving forward is that you step into a new place of freedom. For generations the children of Israel had lived in slavery in Egypt, but in that moment of walking forward they walked right into freedom.

Thus the LORD saved Israel that day from the hand of the Egyptians, and Israel saw the Egyptians dead on the seashore. Exodus 14:30

Regardless of the condition of the place in which you now find yourself, you do not have to stay there. You can move forward into a new place of freedom. God desires to see us move forward and progress in His Spirit to new places in Him (2 Corinthians 3:17-18). This is an ongoing and cyclical process. Once you arrive at the new place of freedom, it establishes a new place of faith, which becomes your new starting point for another step forward into a new freedom, and so the cycle continues. It is a lifelong process. Each of us has to take the steps on our own and at our own speed. I encourage you to move forward. With each step

Josiah took, he brought about a new freedom not only for himself but for all those under his reign. Your steps forward will impact your family, friends, neighbors, and co-workers - everyone in your life. As we move forward from faith into freedom, we find ourselves becoming more and more fruitful. God's process is perfect. Revival brings that into focus and keeps us in step with Him.

Success by Succession

He did right in the sight of the LORD, and walked in the ways of his father David and did not turn aside to the right or to the left.
2 Chronicles 34:2

Another key component of success is following the lead of those before us who have walked in the ways of the Lord. Josiah walked in the ways of his father David. David had set a precedent in his life, as both a shepherd and a king, as a man after God's own heart (Acts 13:22). By walking in the ways of David, Josiah was showing that seeking both God's direction and God's favor would be important in his life and reign. Consider the heritage left for Josiah by his biological father and grandfather:

Amon was twenty-two years old when he became king, and he reigned two years in Jerusalem. He did evil in the sight of the LORD as Manasseh his father had done, and Amon sacrificed to all the carved images which his father Manasseh had made, and he served them. Moreover, he did not humble himself before the LORD as his father Manasseh had done, but Amon multiplied guilt. Finally his servants conspired against him and put him to death in his own house. But the people of the land killed all the conspirators against King Amon, and the people of the land made Josiah his son king in his place.
2 Chronicles 33:21-25

Clearly Josiah did not choose to walk in the ways of his father Amon. Amon had chosen to do what was evil in the sight of the Lord and as a result his reign only lasted two years. We discussed in Chapter Two some keys to sustaining revival, and clearly Amon did now follow those keys. Josiah chose not to continue the natural heritage of Amon; instead he embraced the spiritual heritage of David.

Let us recall what David spoke to his son Solomon just prior to David's death.

"As for you, my son Solomon, know the God of your father,
and serve Him with a whole heart and a willing mind; for
the LORD searches all hearts, and understands every intent of
the thoughts. If you seek Him, He will let you find Him; but if
you forsake Him, He will reject you forever. 1 Chronicles 28:9

By his own choices and his life, Josiah fulfills this declaration by David. By choosing to walk in the ways of David, Josiah was declaring that he was choosing to stand with God and find Him and His blessing and favor.

We all have both a natural and a spiritual heritage that we can choose to follow. There are inclinations to go a certain way and do certain things based on the way paved by those who have gone before us. Yet from this story of Josiah we can understand that we are not obligated to follow any certain path, but we can choose the path of succession for our lives. When Josiah made the choice to follow the ways of David, he was choosing to follow God and to "walk not after the flesh, but after the Spirit" (Romans 8:4).

Who is your influence in life? A perusing of the Bible gives us examples of individuals who were influenced toward success. Joshua was ready to lead because of the lessons he learned from Moses. Elijah trained and prepared Elisha to assume the role he vacated when God caught him away in a chariot of fire. Jesus trained twelve men who would follow in His ways and impact the world. It was these disciples that Jesus originally called to go and bear fruit that would last. Paul trained Timothy from a young age and helped him to become a strong leader within the early church.

It was not uncommon to hear the leaders of the Brownsville revival speak about the influence that Leonard Ravenhill had on their lives. They would speak about how his heart and passion for God was both contagious and inspiring. His book *Why Revival Tarries* has impacted thousands of people. In fact, I have personally made that book a must read for the leadership team of our church.

I consider myself to be extremely blessed in terms of the great men and women of God who have had a direct impact on my life. Who I am today I owe in large part to these individuals. One person who had a profound impact on my life was my father. In him I saw the difference that God can make in a person's life. I remember going to the meetings while he was in an alcohol rehabilitation program. I remember being around when he was gambling away his hard earned money. It would have been very easy for me to follow those ways and allow them to be the shaping heritage for my life. Instead I have chosen to follow the ways of God which my father embraced later on in his own life. These are some invaluable things I learned from my father: his drive and determination to always do his best. His ability to produce so much with so little is a testament to his strength and perseverance. When we buried my father in 2006, we buried a man who taught all eight of his children the importance of being an individual who knew how to make the most of their circumstances. A few weeks later when I assumed my first senior pastor position, I preached from my father's personal Bible – which he had read from daily.

We have the capacity to choose who or what shapes who we become. Revival is the heritage of God's people. Revival is not only about what God does in you, but also what God can do through you to impact others. I want to surround myself with people who have a positive spiritual influence on my life. I also want to surround myself with people who will allow me to have a positive spiritual influence on their lives. I have set my personal definition of success as having a positive impact and influence on every person in my life. And I want that impact to increase the closer I am to the individual. I want to leave a godly legacy. When my son grows up I want it to be said about him that he chose to walk in the ways of his father Rodney.

Let me close Chapter Three with a thought. After Moses led the children of Israel to the brink of the Promised Land, Joshua succeeded him. Under Joshua's leadership the people conquered other nations and took possession of their inheritance. Who did Joshua train to lead in his stead? The answer: he did not train anyone. While godly succession can sustain success, the lack of such succession can be devastating. Look at what happened following Joshua's death:

The people served the LORD all the days of Joshua, and all the days of the elders who survived Joshua, who had seen all the great work of the LORD which He had done for Israel. Then Joshua the son of Nun, the servant of the LORD, died at the age of one hundred and ten. And they buried him in the territory of his inheritance in Timnath-heres, in the hill country of Ephraim, north of Mount Gaash. All that generation also were gathered to their fathers; and there arose another generation after them who did not know the LORD, nor yet the work which He had done for Israel. Then the sons of Israel did evil in the sight of the LORD and served the Baals, and they forsook the LORD, the God of their fathers, who had brought them out of the land of Egypt, and followed other gods from among the gods of the peoples who were around them, and bowed themselves down to them; thus they provoked the LORD to anger. So they forsook the LORD and served Baal and the Ashtaroth. Judges 2:7-13

Let us make sure that we do not allow the chain of succession to be broken. May each of us not only have mentors and coaches in our lives, but also mentor and coach others to keep the succession alive.

Chapter 4 – Focusing on God

He did right in the sight of the LORD, and walked in the ways of his father David and did not turn aside to the right or to the left. For in the eighth year of his reign while he was still a youth, he began to seek the God of his father David; and in the twelfth year he began to purge Judah and Jerusalem of the high places, the Asherim, the carved images and the molten images. 2 Chronicles 34:2-3

Keeping Focused

Josiah did what was right in the eyes of the Lord as he followed the precedent set by David. I am sure there were many distractions that arose during his reign, yet the Bible declares that he did not turn aside to the right or to the left. Josiah stayed focused on his call and purpose. It is vitally important for us to stay focused as we experience revival and the realization of God's plan for our lives. Being able to prioritize and value what is important will become even more necessary when God is moving in your life.

The primary reason for Josiah's success and the revival experienced by he and the people under his reign was that he sought God. Before we cover that I want us to spend some time in the area of being focused. If you cannot be focused and steady outside of revival you definitely will not when revival breaks out in your life. The focus that Josiah showed throughout his reign both set the stage for and sustained what God did.

What are your priorities? What is important will get done. Do you recognize when things are not important? Do you know the difference between urgent and not urgent? Do you control your calendar or does your calendar control you? What fills your free time? These questions are important. We were created by God on purpose and with a purpose and our lives need to be focused on not only finding that purpose, but walking it out in our lives as well. I see far too many people who wander through life seemingly without a clue as to why they are here.

The prophet Jeremiah declared some important truths that we need to latch onto:

"Before I formed you in the womb I knew you, and before you were born I consecrated you; I have appointed you a prophet to the nations." Jeremiah 1:5

For I know the plans that I have for you,' declares the LORD, 'plans for welfare and not for calamity to give you a future and a hope. Jeremiah 29:11

Jeremiah prophesied during the reign of Josiah. I wonder if Josiah had these words carved into the stone wall of his bedroom. He understood that he had a destiny and he walked in that destiny with focus and resolve.

What things distract you or keep you from being focused? Let's consider some distractions that may present themselves to try to steal our focus.

1. Busyness

Being busy is not the same as being effective. It is not difficult to fill a daily or weekly to-do list. There are plenty of things that can be done on a day to day basis. A focused individual will learn the difference between what can be done and what needs to be done. I am not advocating giving up your responsibilities. What I am talking about is not allowing the non-important to take precedence over the important. Plus, if you are in a position to do so, learn to delegate responsibilities. If you are like me that is difficult. Oftentimes my mindset is that there is no need to ask someone else to do what I can do myself. But what benefit is there in completing tasks at the expense of really making progress? The best example we have of proper delegation is in Acts 6 where we are told about the selection of elders.

So the twelve summoned the congregation of the disciples and said, "It is not desirable for us to neglect the word of God in order to serve tables. Therefore, brethren, select from among you seven men of good reputation, full of the Spirit and of wisdom, whom we may put in charge of this task. But we will devote ourselves to prayer and to the ministry of the word." Acts 6:2-4

What was requested of the disciples was worthwhile and important. But the disciples stood strong in what was their true purpose. When you know your purpose you must be focused on completing it. Do not allow busyness to steal from your effectiveness. In Chapter Seven we will cover the importance of delegating responsibility in greater detail.

2. Idleness/Wasting Time

On the other side of busyness we find idleness. This typically manifests itself in the mundane things we do that are basically time wasters. Now, I am a proponent of having a hobby and having some down time, although I do not always excel at either. But if we are not careful we can spend far too much time is these things. Idle time truly can be the devil's workshop. At creation we read that God rested on the seventh day. But at creation we also clearly see the focus God had the other six days.

So many quickly lose their focus on what they need to be doing by becoming idle or by getting involved in time wasting activities. Have you noticed how quickly time can pass in front of the television or at the computer? Men, how much time can we allow to slip away by simply thinking about nothing? I find the longer I lose focus and waste time the harder it is to get back on track.

3. *Something Shiny*

Whenever I get focused on something, if I allow myself to get distracted by something else I know I am in trouble. It amazes me how quickly I can turn my attention from one thing to another. Sometimes the shiny thing is urgent; sometimes it is just shiny. Either way it can be a barrier to progress. Do you remember Achan's sin that caused Israel to lose the battle against Ai? The entire army of Israel had been given a mission to go into Jericho and completely destroy the city. God had told them to take nothing for themselves. The army was focused. Yet, Achan was attracted to something shiny.

So Achan answered Joshua and said, "Truly, I have sinned against the LORD, the God of Israel, and this is what I did: when I saw among the spoil a beautiful mantle from Shinar and two hundred shekels of silver and a bar of gold fifty shekels in weight, then I coveted them and took them; and behold, they are concealed in the earth inside my tent with the silver underneath it." Joshua 7:20-21

It was a visual distraction for Achan; it took place when he *saw*. We can so easily become distracted by what is attractive to us. A horse is often trained with blinders on the sides of his head to keep him from being spooked or thrown off course by what gets in his line of sight. God help us to have blinders on to the things that would steal our focus. This is so important. Just like in the story of Achan, his decision to be distracted impacted more than just him. When we lose focus it affects those who are counting on us.

4. Pride

Pride can become a major distraction as it causes us to focus on ourselves. A person can so quickly become enamored with self and feel as though any and all success is because of them. Philippians Chapter Two clearly describes the attitude and approach we must have. We are not to think only about ourselves but to esteem others. We are called to have the same mind as Christ, who came as a servant and carried out His purpose in humility.

Revival sets a stage on which pride loves to perform. When God is moving it can become so easy to start to focus on self and take the credit that belongs to God. *"Look What the Lord Has Done"* was an anthem often sung during the Brownsville revival. If we allow pride to creep in, we could find ourselves changing the words to "Look at the Works I've Done." I can remember thinking that since I was a part of the revival and served on the prayer team that somehow made me important. I often found myself walking past people and thinking to myself, "I am sure they felt the anointing just then." Pride can move in so quickly. Those thoughts and feelings are a big reason that I went through a season where the anointing of God was dormant in my life. The stirring up of the gift in my own life that I recounted in Chapter One also came with a reminder to stay humble before the Lord.

Generally pride creeps in when we allow ourselves to become dissatisfied or discontent with the place in which we find ourselves. Pride is ultimately what brought about the downfall of Nimrod as he was trying to make a name for himself. Satan worked in him to cause him to desire a position of prominence that did not belong to him, and from that time he has been using that tool to deceive many. Isaiah describes it this way:

"How you have fallen from heaven, O star of the morning, son of the dawn! You have been cut down to the earth, you who have weakened the nations! "But you said in your heart, 'I will ascend to heaven; I will raise my throne above the stars of God, and I will sit on the mount of assembly in the recesses of the north. 'I will ascend above the heights of the clouds; I will make myself like the Most High.' "Nevertheless you will be thrust down to Sheol, to the recesses of the pit.
Isaiah 14:12-15

Lucifer himself even determined in his heart that he deserved better than the place he found himself, and that he deserved more credit and praise. The Bible lists three angels known as archangels – Michael, Gabriel and Lucifer. Lucifer was part of a select group. He had a position of importance and esteem. Yet it was not enough for him. He was not content to be one of three. He wanted to be number one.

Let us always stay on our guard and protect against the invasion of pride. Pride can quickly get our focus off of what we are called to do and onto self.

5. Self-Doubt

Self-doubt is typically the antithesis of pride, but it can be just as damaging. Questioning or doubting who we are in Christ can be debilitating. Many have come to a complete stop in their lives because they failed to see themselves as God sees them. Earlier in this chapter we considered how God spoke to Jeremiah that before he was formed in his mother's womb God knew him and appointed him. (Not one human mistake has ever been born.) While a person's biological parents may not have planned for the pregnancy that brought a person into this world, God created each of us on purpose and with a purpose.

It is so critical that we learn to understand this truth - Jesus loves you and God has a plan for your life. I pray those words are like arrows that pierce each of our hearts and help us find a place of focus and resolve that drives us to succeed in Christ. God's need from each of us is not our ability but rather our availability. When we become focused on His purpose for our lives and get about the Father's business, there is no room for self-doubt, because it is not about us anyway.

In my attempts to steer clear of the pitfall of pride that I fell into previously, I sometimes teeter in the area of self-doubt. It is really a balance; the lines between self-doubt and pride are not that far apart. There are times, however, that the enemy of our souls will work hard to try and cause us to second guess our usefulness to God. There are also times when we can do well enough with self-doubt that Satan does not need to help with that at all.

Consider Moses. We view him as a great man of God and a great leader of God's people. But even Moses almost lost his opportunity at greatness. God appeared to him at the burning bush and called him to lead the children of Israel out of their place of slavery in Egypt. God laid out for Moses the plan and what he was to say to ensure the people that God had truly sent him. In spite of all this, Moses hesitated and questioned because of self-doubt. Look at his conversation with God:

Then Moses said to the LORD, "Please, Lord, I have never been eloquent, neither recently nor in time past, nor since You have spoken to Your servant; for I am slow of speech and slow of tongue." The LORD said to him, "Who has made man's mouth? Or who makes him mute or deaf, or seeing or blind? Is it not I, the LORD? Now then go, and I, even I, will be with your mouth, and teach you what you are to say." But he said, "Please, Lord, now send the message by whomever You will." Exodus 4:10-13

Can you picture this? God had hand-picked Moses for this assignment and he was trying to convince God he was not qualified. Leonard Ravenhill has been quoted as saying, "The opportunity of a lifetime must be seized during the lifetime of the opportunity." But at the burning bush, when an opportunity of a lifetime presented itself, Moses tried to change God's mind because of his own self-doubt. When self-doubt comes in we will say or do just about anything to get out of the situation. Moses had been raised in Pharaoh's family. Do you think he was uneducated or that he did not speak well? Notice what Stephen says about him in Acts,

Moses was educated in all the learning of the Egyptians, and he was a man of power in words and deeds. Acts 7:22

Everything about Moses was right for what God had called him to do. He had been destined for this position. Life had shaped Moses for this season of service. Just like with Moses, God has placed inside of you all that you need to effectively fulfill His purpose for your life. We cannot afford to allow self-doubt to steal away our opportunities. Rise above this tendency, focus on God and what He has called you to do, and go for it.

Seek Him

When our focus is on God and we are keeping our eyes upon Him, there is nothing that we cannot do. The absolute best way to remain focused is by being one who seeks God. Hebrews calls it "fixing our eyes upon Jesus" (Hebrews 12:2). Do you remember what caused Peter to begin to sink as he was walking on the water toward Jesus? The answer: he took his eyes of Jesus.

But seeing the wind, he became frightened, and beginning to sink, he cried out, "Lord, save me!" Matthew 14:30

The moment we lose focus and take our eyes off the Lord is the moment that we begin to sink and lose our effectiveness. One of the greatest pitfalls of revival is that you can so quickly become enamored by the wind and the waves around you that you take your eyes off Jesus. It can easily get to the point that you begin to seek revival more than the Reviver.

Our foundational passage in 2 Chronicles 34 says that Josiah "began to seek the God of his father David" (34:3). This established the foundation for his reign as king. All of his decisions and rulings were impacted by his seeking God. Josiah's role as king flowed out of his relationship with God. When we emphasize our relationship with God, our role in life becomes clear. The problem is that we often elevate our role above our relationship. We live in such a results based society and that can lead a person to do whatever they must to seem productive. We can work so hard on bringing about the things in life that we deem necessary and important. Yet, Jesus taught us to "seek first his kingdom and his righteousness, and all these things will be given to you as well" (Matthew 6:33). If we seek the things we may get the things. If we seek His kingdom we receive His kingdom and the things as well.

At the beginning of this chapter we read from Jeremiah that God knows the plans He has for us (29:11). By reading the next few verses we realize that God desires to be found by us as we fulfill the plan He has for us.

Then you will call upon Me and come and pray to Me, and I will listen to you. You will seek Me and find Me when you search for Me with all your heart. Jeremiah 29:12-13

My son loves to play hide and seek. He impresses me with how well he plays at such a young age. As his father my favorite part of the game is when I hide and he seeks me. Sometimes I hear him say, "Daddy, I am looking for a clue." At that point I want to jump out and grab him in a big hug and exclaim, "Here I am!" It always warms my heart when he finds me. He looks at me with such excitement. Our Father in Heaven is no different toward us. God, however, is not playing a game with us; He is not hidden and unapproachable. He longs to be found by us.

A great pre-cursor and sustainer for revival is the desire to seek and know God. By nature we seek and desire what is important to us. When we seek God we show how important He is in our lives. I want us to consider the how and why of seeking God. This is not a manual of the way to seek God, but a menu of some ways to seek Him.

1. *We seek Him in prayer.*

We have a tendency to make prayer more difficult than it needs to be. Prayer is simply communication with God. Communication indicates that both speaking and listening are involved. We are a blessed creation in that we have the privilege of communicating with our Creator. God is a fan of communicating with you and me. Many books have been written about prayer. Many sermons have been preached about prayer. Many seminars have been hosted about prayer. Prayer is the most talked about, yet probably the least done thing in Christianity. I alluded to *Why Revival Tarries* by Leonard Ravenhill in Chapter Three. Let's look at the opening paragraph of that book.

The Cinderella of the church of today is the prayer meeting. This handmaid of the Lord is unloved and unwooed because she is not dripping with the pearls of intellectualism, nor glamorous with the silks of philosophy; neither is she enchanting with the tiara of psychology. She wears the homespuns of sincerity and humility and is not afraid to kneel! (Ravenhill, 1979, p. 1).

It is not always glamorous to pray. Prayer is such an easy activity during which to be distracted. Nearly every time you go to pray there are sure to be a million tasks of which you are reminded. Let me be practical for a moment. Take a pen and paper with you. When these tasks come to mind write down an after prayer to-do list. That will help to keep you from dwelling on the tasks and losing your focus in prayer. Cell phones do not make good prayer partners either. In your prayer life, learn to have the Lord as your only guest. There are times when praying with others is important, but do not neglect the personal private times of prayer.

When you are in prayer, have you ever wondered what you should pray? The most basic and effective approach for me is to come to the Lord in praise and worship first. This helps me to get my attitude and emotions in the right place for prayer. Typically I will then take some time to listen. What the Lord brings to your heart and mind in prayer are the best things about which to pray. Learning to hear from God is so vital in seeking Him and developing a relationship with Him. If either my wife or I was the only speaker in our marriage, we would not have a very healthy relationship. I figure God gave us two ears and one mouth for a reason. In prayer, learning to use the ears more is a good step.

Before we move into another example of how to seek God, I want to say one more thing about prayer. Do not be afraid to be honest with God. So many people struggle with this practice, but God is neither afraid of nor offended by your honesty. If you are upset or disappointed then tell Him. Holding back from God will often be the final wall that must come down for you to find your victory. Some of my most blessed and effective times of prayer have been when I shared my frustrations with God. When we are honest with God it allows for both Him and us to address the real issue.

2. *We seek Him in His Word.*

We must be teachable students of God's Word. I have read many good books, but the only book that I allow to guide my life is the Bible. The Bible is foundational to Christianity. If we call ourselves a Christian we should place high priority on reading and knowing what God has said.

Learn to incorporate the Word into your prayer life. In fact, if you are having trouble with consistency in prayer and Bible reading (that makes you human) commit to the 5 minute plan. For the next twenty-one days pray for five minutes, listen to God for five minutes, and read the Bible for five minutes. Allow these disciplines to become established in your life. I promise they will make a difference.

One thing I stress to our congregation is the necessity to know God's Word for ourselves. It is neither fair nor healthy if all I know about the Bible is what I have heard in Sunday School or in sermons. Each of us should know and understand what God's Word says to us. On countless occasions I have referred to the church in Berea, whom Paul commended for this very thing.

Now these were more noble-minded than those in Thessalonica, for they received the word with great eagerness, examining the Scriptures daily to see whether these things were so. Acts 17:11

Nobody who teaches or preaches a message is going to be 100% accurate 100% of the time. Each will make a mistake. Some will purposefully try and lead others astray. How would we ever know the difference without knowing the Bible for ourselves? Some of my favorite moments in ministry have been when someone in the congregation has questioned something I said during a sermon. It did not bother me in the least; actually, it thrilled me. It told me that the individual was paying attention and it told me that they were learning and knowing the Word for themselves.

And when you read the Bible, read it for formation and not just for information. Allow God's Word to have an impact on your life. The Bible is not just some history book. It is not a fairy tale. The Bible is God's Word. Without God's Word in our lives we will be anemic Christians.

All Scripture is inspired by God and profitable for teaching, for reproof, for correction, for training in righteousness; so that the man of God may be adequate, equipped for every good work.
2 Timothy 3:16-17

3. We seek Him in worship.

I must admit this is my favorite way to seek God. I absolutely love worship. Very few things get me as excited as focusing on how good God is and celebrating that in worship. I also love that there is no formula or cookie-cutter approach to worship. Worship must be done for the eyes of the Lord – He is our audience. I do, however, enjoy watching the different ways that people respond to God in worship. I am a jumper and a dancer in worship. I get physically involved in worship. My wife is a quiet, eyes closed, lost in her own world worshiper. Neither is wrong. Worship must genuinely flow from who you are. Worship is not about the posture of your body; worship is about the posture of your heart. When we open our hearts before the Lord in worship we are seeking Him in a very intimate way.

I am an avid sports fan. I thoroughly enjoy watching a good ballgame. I have a high level of respect for the skill shown by the athletes involved. In particular, it was always thrilling to me to watch Michael Jordan play basketball. He had worked so hard to hone his skills and he played the game the right way. I know facts and details about Mr. Jordan – most of which I learned from the back of a basketball card. If he were to walk in the room, I would be excited and perhaps even a little giddy. But I would not be able to go over and carry on a conversation with him, because I do not know him. On the other hand, when I am in a time of worship and the Lord of Heaven comes into the room I do not just get excited and giddy; I get as close to Him as I can and worship Him and communicate with Him in a real way. I know Him and I worship Him out of a desire to know Him more.

Jesus taught that "God is spirit, and his worshipers must worship in the Spirit and in truth" (John 4:24). In spirit is the level at which true worship takes place. In truth involves the truth of the Father, revealed in the Son, and received through the Spirit because truth is God's very nature and characteristic. True worship is done out of reverence for Who God is. We worship God because of how great He truly is. True worship is a sacrifice unto God. When Abraham was taking his son Isaac up the mountain to sacrifice him in obedience to God, he called it worship (Genesis 22:2-5). True worship is also undignified. King David danced and worshiped before the Lord as the Ark of the Covenant was being returned to Jerusalem. When Michal his wife confronted him, he responded that he would become even more undignified in his worship to God (2 Samuel 6:20-22).

May we all be those who seek God through the avenues of prayer, reading and studying His Word and worship. May these become ongoing disciplines in our lives – shaping who we become in Christ. But not only is it important to consider some ways to seek Him, we must also understand why we seek Him.

4. We seek Him because of Who He is.

I do not want to spend my life seeking God because of the good things He has done or can do for me. I want to spend my life seeking God because of who He is. If God never does another thing for me in my life, I still have plenty of reasons to thank and seek Him – the main reason being that He is God. I do not want to get wrapped up seeking the blessings of God more than I seek the God of the blessings. Our motives for seeking Him must not be selfish and with an agenda. He desires us to seek Him simply because He is God.

As the Brownsville revival was taking place, and as revival was spreading and taking place in other parts of the country and around the world, it became very easy to make revival the focus. It became very commonplace to find people and churches seeking revival. What the world saw in Pensacola was a result of a group of people seeking God in their lives and on behalf of their church. But what took place in Pensacola may not be right for the context in which you find yourself.

Those who have experienced the most with and from God, however, have been those who have made it a point to seek God and not to seek revival. As we seek God, He knows best what it is that we have need of in our lives, our churches, and our communities. By seeking Him and not what we assume revival is, we are asking Him to come and do what it is that He desires to do and knows needs to be done within our context

Let us close out this chapter by once again considering Jeremiah 29.

You will seek Me and find Me when you search for Me with all your heart. Jeremiah 29:13

As we do the things mentioned in this chapter: as we keep our relationship with God in proper focus, as we keep ourselves from becoming distracted or led away by the things around us, as we seek God for who He is and not for what He does, all the good that He has in store for us in His presence will be realized.

Chapter 5 – Purging the Land

In the twelfth year he began to purge Judah and Jerusalem of the high places, the Asherim, the carved images and the molten images. They tore down the altars of the Baals in his presence, and the incense altars that were high above them he chopped down; also the Asherim, the carved images and the molten images he broke in pieces and ground to powder and scattered it on the graves of those who had sacrificed to them. Then he burned the bones of the priests on their altars and purged Judah and Jerusalem. In the cities of Manasseh, Ephraim, Simeon, even as far as Naphtali, in their surrounding ruins.   2 Chronicles 34:3-6

Revival Brings Cleansing

In Chapter Four we discussed the importance of staying focused and seeking God.   Those important characteristics of revival are sure to bring a renewed sense of God's presence, which is sure to bring a renewed sense of our sin and the need for purging. Because Josiah had made it a point to seek God and follow His ways, the need to purge Israel of the sin in the land became clear. As we explored in Chapter One, as Solomon was dedicating the temple he declared the recipe for seeing healing brought to the land (see 2 Chronicles 7). As king, Josiah saw a nation turn from the wicked ways which had caused desolation and destruction for so many years.

One of the hallmarks of the Brownsville Revival was the emphasis on repentance. Each service was marked by a powerful altar call that, during the five year span of the revival, saw countless thousands respond in repentance. Never before nor since have I personally heard someone give a more impassioned altar call than Evangelist Steve Hill. Every night I would stand in amazement watching men and women of all ages literally run to an altar to allow God to purge the sin in their lives. I was watching God's Word play out in front of me, because throughout Scripture God's presence would lay the sinner bare before Him. That is the fruit of revival.

Without repentance, purging, and a people "turning from their wicked ways," (2 Chronicles 7:14) what you have is a refreshing for the people of God. There is nothing wrong with refreshing, and I love the many times that God has allowed me to enjoy the refreshing of His Spirit. Even Peter declared in Acts that "times of refreshing" would come (Acts 3:19). True revival, however, is marked by a purging of sin in individuals and even in societies. Frank Bartleman is quoted as saying, "The depth of your repentance determines the height of your revival." We find evidence in this recounting of revival in America during the early 1900s:

"Revival spread quickly from Pennsylvania to New Jersey. In Atlantic City, not more than fifty unconverted people were reported to be remaining in a population of sixty thousand" (Duewel, 1995, p. 209).

What a mark of revival! When God is moving people will repent and be born again. Revival should have a lasting impact in the city and on the society in which it is occurring. "Revival does what human programs and campaigns, though well intended, cannot do" (Duewel, 212). We cannot schedule or force God's presence, but *when* revival comes it brings purging and forgiveness. To purge indicates to clean physically, ceremonially, and morally. During the reign of Josiah the land was purged. Let us consider the purging that Josiah saw in his day.

What Was Purged

1. High Places

The high places were set up under Jeroboam so that the people would not return to Jerusalem to worship God as He had designed. They represented man's attempt to worship God on his own terms. It was man's way of saying not to worry about worshiping the way God said to worship. Right can become wrong when done in disobedience or with wrong motives. Josiah broke down the high places, because God does have a design for how we worship.

Revival is about God bringing His people and His church back into alignment with His design. While we may not journey to high places for worship, are there practices in our lives and churches that do not line up with God's design? Revival is about God restoring His house to its intended purpose. I love the image we find in Matthew when Jesus cleansed the temple.

And Jesus entered the temple and drove out all those who were buying and selling in the temple, and overturned the tables of the money changers and the seats of those who were selling doves. And He said to them, "It is written, 'My house shall be called a house of prayer'; but you are making it a robber's den." And the blind and the lame came to Him in the temple, and He healed them. But when the chief priests and the scribes saw the wonderful things that He had done, and the children who were shouting in the temple, "Hosanna to the Son of David," they became indignant and said to Him, "Do You hear what these children are saying?" And Jesus *said to them, "Yes; have you never read, 'Out of the mouth of infants and nursing babies you have prepared praise for

*yourself'?" And He left them and went out of the city
to Bethany, and spent the night there. Matthew 21:12-17*

In this passage we find the passion God has for His house and how He desires to see order restored – by bringing revival. Much of the church has assumed ownership and authority of God's House, and used His House in a way that best suits her own needs and her own kingdom. Consider what we see Jesus restoring to His house in this passage in Matthew.

Jesus Restored His Presence

Jesus went into the temple. Let us not take that for granted. In how many temples today is He welcome to enter? There are churches that function week after week without His presence. The high places, or our own terms of worship, have been set up as we like them.

For many it is about having a God who fits within their ideology or expectations. Tommy Tenney once said, "God often has to tone down His presence to meet our expectation." The religious reaction to the presence of Jesus has been the same for centuries. Many want a god or a religion that they can understand and control. God wants to restore His presence among His people.

Jesus Restored Prayer

Jesus declared that God's House was to be a house of prayer. In Chapter Four we discussed how we seek God in prayer. When God sent revival to Brownsville Assembly of God on Father's Day 1995, it was largely in response to prayer. Two and a half years before Father's Day, Pastor John Kilpatrick had instituted a Sunday evening prayer service in lieu of their normal Sunday night service. As the church made prayer a priority, God's presence came in a powerful way.

Nothing moves God like prayer. Not our programs, our facilities, not the quality of those things, or the people behind them. God has always and will always respond to sincere prayer. We desperately need a restoration of prayer in God's house. From pulpit to pew, prayer must be a priority. If our way of doing church is without prayer, we have missed God's design and we will miss God's presence. I heard of a pastor once commenting that his church had tried the prayer thing and it did not work. God help us not to exchange prayer for activities that appear more glamorous or effective.

Jesus Restored Power

It has always been interesting to me that healing and the display of God's power came on the heels of the cleansing of the temple. Having condemned those things that did not belong, Jesus quickly shows what should be taking place in God's House.

Jesus restored vision to those who were not able to see. The implication here is a restoration of not only physical vision but spiritual vision as well. We need to catch a glimpse of our Savior once again, and capture His heart and vision for His church. Proverbs warns us that without vision the people perish (Proverb 29:18).

Jesus healed the lame – He gave mobility back to the church. Religion and the high places that we fashion will bring about stagnation. By healing the lame, Jesus was indicating the importance for the church to again be active and mobile .

Jesus Restored Praise

This praise was exuberant and sincere: *the children shouting in the temple courts, "Hosanna to the Son of David."* How often do we rush through or tone down our praise? How often do we forget the power of praise? Take a look at a powerful truth concerning praise:

From the lips of children and infants you have ordained praise because of your enemies, to silence the foe and the avenger.
Psalm 8:2 (NIV)

Praise unto God will silence the foe and avenger. What a powerful truth. Yet how many of us sit distracted during times of praise at church or even fail to praise at all in our lives? By not choosing to praise, we are saying that we would rather listen to what our foe has to say. I do not like the lies the enemy speaks. I do not want to spend my life listening to him. Therefore, I am going to be a person of praise so as to silence his voice!

Some translations substitute the word "strength" for "praise." The strength that we need comes from the praise of our lips. They are interchangeable. Perhaps a primary reason many are weak is due to a lack of praise in their hearts and in their lives.

Setting up the high places is man's way of telling God how he will approach Him. When this was put into place by Jeroboam it led to years of disunity, disappointment, and trouble. Anytime we choose to go against God's plan, we will forfeit God's best (Deuteronomy 28). Like Josiah, let us tear down the high places and get back to worshiping God as He has designed.

2. Asherah Poles

Asherah poles or groves were manufactured forms of fortune and happiness, representing man's attempt to gain these blessings on their own terms. How often do we try and manufacture in our own way what God has already promised to give us freely?

God's desire is to bless us as we walk in accordance with His plan. We have been created in the image of God as three part beings – spirit, soul, and body. God created our spirit first; He made us out of nothing that had previously existed, forming our spirit in His image. Our bodies were made out of the dust of the ground as a vehicle that would house our spirit. Our soul is our conscience, mind, will, and emotions; it is the connecting point between our spirit and body, the essence of who we are. As God has designed, we are spirit, soul, and body – in that order. We cause problems in our lives when we get this out of order. Society places the emphasis on body instead of spirit. This prioritizes things in direct opposition to God's design, which always brings about heavy consequences. Moses warned us about this:

"But it shall come about, if you do not obey the LORD your God, to observe to do all His commandments and His statutes with which I charge you today, that all these curses will come upon you and overtake you:" Deuteronomy 28:15

This warning is followed up by a long list of the curses God will bring in response to disobedience. While the Asherah poles represent our effort to manufacture what God has promised to give us freely, in reality they serve to align us with God's curses and not His blessings.

3. Idols

An idol is anything that takes the place of God, and at its core it is man creating god in his own image: a god that man can understand, manipulate, and fashion. Idolatry is really the core of religion. Religion is popular because it allows you to shape a god in your own image. Christianity, on the other hand, is about the God of Heaven shaping us into His image. Idolatry happens because many prefer to be the shaper rather than the one being shaped. It ultimately boils down to control. If we can fashion our own object of worship then we can dictate the amount of control our god has in our lives.

Idolatry is not always blatant, but can work in subtle ways as well. What things in our lives do we give higher priority than God? A dangerous pitfall for those involved in ministry is to place ministry on the throne. How often have servants of God fell victim to this form of idolatry? God never intended for what we do to become more important than who we are.

In my own life I must constantly remind myself of priorities to ensure that I do not allow idolatry to become my own undoing. First and foremost, I am a Christian. My number one focus is on being a man of God. Secondly, I am a husband. It would be 100% wrong of me to allow my wife to become more important than my relationship with God, but to put anything other than my relationship with God ahead of my wife is equally as wrong. Third, I am a father. As much as I love my son, I cannot allow him to become an idol in my life. It would be unhealthy for him and for me. Fourthly, I am a pastor. The danger is to flip this order and make it about the ministry to which God has called me. That is yet another form of idolatry.

4. *Altars of Baal*

Here we find that altars were destroyed – plural. More than one altar had been set up unto Baal. Is it possible that this was man's attempt to copy what God had established? Consider the tabernacle of Moses and the temple of Solomon. There was the altar of burnt offering (Exodus 30:28), the brazen altar placed in the outer court (Exodus 39:39), and the altar of incense or golden altar within the temple (Exodus 30:27; 1 Kings 7:48).

When the enemy counterfeits something of God, it is typically as close to genuine as possible. In some ways, the deception is so well done that many cannot tell the difference. The altars of Baal had been in place for so long that the people had accepted them as not only normal but genuine. It is a dangerous thing to live with sin long enough that you become comfortable with it.

The altars of Baal represent the epitome of false religion. It resembled God's way just enough to be attractive and acceptable. It was an early example of the antichrist. In fact, the way of the antichrist has been paved for centuries, and the closer we get to his coming, the more acceptable he is becoming. John said this about the antichrist.

Beloved, do not believe every spirit, but test the spirits to see whether they are from God, because many false prophets have gone out into the world. By this you know the Spirit of God: every spirit that confesses that Jesus Christ has come in the flesh is from God; and every spirit that does not confess Jesus is not from God; this is the spirit of the antichrist, of which you have heard that it is coming, and now it is already in the world. 1 John 4:1-3

Here John teaches that the spirit of the antichrist is already in the world and working to deceive. The ultimate plan for the antichrist is to counterfeit all that Christ taught and stood for, and to cause people to accept him as the real Christ. The setting up of the altars of Baal was an early form of this very deception. The enemy loves to deceive us by setting up what appears to be right. If he can get us to take our eyes off of Christ and instead get our eyes on him, he will be successful in derailing God's destiny in our lives. His intent is to distort, to deceive, and to destroy. Let us be on our guard and not bow to any altar other than the altar of God.

Standing for Truth

It is important to note that our passage says these things took place "under his (Josiah's) direction" (v 4). God has always chosen to work through man, and He will establish godly leadership for revival. It is so important to have leaders that will properly confront sin and wickedness. The bottom line is that in terms of sin, neither your opinion nor my opinion is all that important. What really matters is what God says. The real issue is not standing *against sin*, but rather standing *for truth*. Listen to these words from Steve Hill in his book *White Cane Religion*:

Pastors, John the Baptist told the Jews the ugly truth and they flocked to him in repentance. America knows where it stands – don't try to lie to Americans. You can tell them God loves them all day long, but they want to hear about judgment. They want to know the truthful answers to the question, "Am I going to make it to Heaven?" You need to tell them, "You're going to go to hell in your sin if you don't repent and ask Jesus for

mercy!" The people in John's day had seen all the religious hypocrisy. They had heard all the "pillow prophets" lulling them to sleep with religious sweet nothings. Then they heard hard-preaching John the Baptist say, "You brood of vipers, you have come to be baptized, but if you don't start bearing good fruit for the Kingdom of God, the ax is already laid to the root! The Messiah will chop you down and cut you to ribbons." So why did they follow such a no-nonsense, "narrow-minded" preacher? The hearts of the people bore witness to the truth!
(Hill, 1997, p. 163).

Josiah took his purpose and position very seriously. During Josiah's reign, the Prophet Jeremiah uttered these words:

Then the LORD stretched out His hand and touched my mouth, and the LORD said to me, "Behold, I have put My words in your mouth. "See, I have appointed you this day over the nations and over the kingdoms, to pluck up and to break down, to destroy and to overthrow, to build and to plant."
Jeremiah 1:9-10

God placed Josiah upon the throne with a purpose, and Josiah understood that his ultimate purpose was not to build his own kingdom or to establish or improve his image. Josiah was there to glorify God and make His Name known among the people once again. What is said about your life today? What is it that is taking place under your direction? Are you building, establishing, and strengthening your own kingdom? Are you working to preserve and protect your name and image? Or, like Josiah, are you standing for truth in the midst of sin?

So many times people believe that they have to arrive at some special place for God to use them. What is important for us to understand, however, is that God is able to help us become what He wants and needs us to be. Josiah was one of many men who served as king. Assuming the throne did not automatically make him someone special. But the way he served throughout his reign is what set him apart. God is able to help you grow in the midst of your service. If we will allow God to do His work in our lives, He will be able to do His work through our lives. Then we will see great things accomplished for His Kingdom.

Dealing with Sin Aggressively

In addition to his standing for truth, we find that Josiah dealt with the sin in the land very aggressively. Churches and church leaders can get themselves in trouble by choosing to deal passively with sin. Paul taught the Corinthians:

For though we walk in the flesh, we do not war according to the flesh, for the weapons of our warfare are not of the flesh, but divinely powerful for the destruction of fortresses. We are destroying speculations and every lofty thing raised up against the knowledge of God, and we are taking every thought captive to the obedience of Christ.
2 Corinthians 10:3-5

It is imperative that we deal with anything that would steal away from God and His plan in and for our lives. The people under Josiah's reign saw a great revival. Had Josiah chosen not to deal with the sin that was present, however, the revival would have been short lived. I for one do not want to do or allow anything that would grieve God's Spirit and possibly cause His presence to be lifted.

Consider our foundational passage again and look at how Josiah dealt with the sin:

In the twelfth year he began to purge Judah and Jerusalem of the high places, the Asherim, the carved images and the molten images. They tore down the altars of the Baals in his presence, and the incense altars that were high above them he chopped down; also the Asherim, the carved images and the molten images he broke in pieces and ground to powder and scattered it on the graves of those who had sacrificed to them. Then he burned the bones of the priests on their altars and purged Judah and Jerusalem. In the cities of Manasseh, Ephraim, Simeon, even as far as Naphtali, in their surrounding ruins, he also tore down the altars and beat the Asherim and the carved images into powder, and chopped down all the incense altars throughout the land of Israel. Then he returned to Jerusalem. 2 Chronicles 34:3-7

Josiah dealt with sin violently. Look at the words used to describe his actions: He tore down, cut to pieces, smashed, broke, and scattered everything that represented the sin in the land. He burned the bones of the priests who had led the people in their sin, and he crushed the idols to powder throughout Israel. He was not slapping someone on the wrist for doing badly. Josiah aggressively went after the kingdom of darkness so as to allow God's light to shine in the land. Josiah was fulfilling his prophetic destiny (see 1 Kings 13).

We cannot afford to play games with sin. Iniquity and sin will separate us from God (Isaiah 59:2); to allow sin to remain is to imply that we are better off separated from God. "Two thousand years ago, Heaven stormed hell in an all-out attack and won. Jesus waged violent warfare to save the entire race of imprisoned mankind" (Hill, 1997, p. 164). The examples of both Josiah and Jesus highlight the importance of dealing aggressively with sin. Jesus Himself declared "*the kingdom of heaven suffereth violence, and the violent take it by force" (Matthew 11:12).* May the sustaining of revival be so important to us that we stand for truth and against sin.

Exposing the Promoters of the False

From the beginning, Satan has tried to infiltrate society with sin and disobedience to God's Word. He has often tried to counterfeit God's plan by using individuals to promote sin. Jude wrote in his letter concerning these people:

For certain persons have crept in unnoticed, those who were long beforehand marked out for this condemnation, ungodly persons who turn the grace of our God into licentiousness and deny our only Master and Lord, Jesus Christ. Jude 1:4

Josiah burned the bones of the priests on their altars. Not only did he deal aggressively with the sin in the land, he also dealt aggressively with those who had promoted sin. Josiah dealt with these priests in the same way that Elijah dealt with the prophets of Baal (see 1 Kings 18-19). False prophets must be dealt with lest they lead many to rebellion and disobedience. Had Josiah not dealt with the priests it would have been an approval of all for which they stood.

Ultimately what must be done is the exposing of all that is false – false teaching, false religion, and false prophecy. Not only has God called us to avoid sin, but we are called to expose sin for what it is. Consider what God teaches us in Ephesians:

For you were formerly darkness, but now you are Light in the Lord; walk as children of Light (for the fruit of the Light consists in all goodness and righteousness and truth), trying to learn what is pleasing to the Lord. Do not participate in the

unfruitful deeds of darkness, but instead even expose them.
Ephesians 5:8-11

In Chapter Three we discussed how righteousness is the fruit of revival, and how God desires for us to produce fruit that remains. The deeds of darkness are called fruitless. Sin has no lasting positive value. It will take you further than you want to go, cost you more than you want to pay, and keep you longer than you want to stay. If we desire revival – a move of God – we must be willing to confront the sin in our lives and in our world.

By burning the bones of the priests, Josiah was exposing the destructive nature of sin. It was not that he was going after individuals as much as he was going after that for which those individuals stood. God Himself is the ultimate Judge of those who practice sin. It is our responsibility to protect God's truth and expose falsehood.

Since Josiah was so intent on following God's ways and standing for His truth, he had no choice but to confront the sin in the land. The purging of the land was a by-product of his commitment to God. As we draw closer to God in revival it will become necessary for us to "have nothing to do with the fruitless deeds of darkness, but rather expose them" (Ephesians 5:11).

God's plan has always involved His Kingdom becoming real in and through the lives of His people. In Chapter Six we will look at how revival spreads to impact beyond its starting point. But to close out this chapter I want us to consider just how serious God is about us doing our part to see sin purged from the land we possess.

But if you do not drive out the inhabitants of the land from before you, then it shall come about that those whom you let remain of them will become as pricks in your eyes and as thorns in your sides, and they will trouble you in the land in which you live. And as I plan to do to them, so I will do to you.'" Numbers 33:55-56

Josiah took this concept quite seriously. He was not willing to allow the inhabitants of the land – physical or spiritual – to remain and oppose what God was doing. Let us, like him, take the purging of the land seriously.

Chapter 6 – The Spread of Revival

In the cities of Manasseh, Ephraim, Simeon, even as far as Naphtali, in their surrounding ruins, he also tore down the altars and beat the Asherim and the carved images into powder, and chopped down all the incense altars throughout the land of Israel. Then he returned to Jerusalem.
2 Chronicles 34:6-7

The Spread of Revival

Revival spread beyond Jerusalem. While revival will generally have a starting place, it is not God's intention for revival to remain in only one location. God desires for His presence to spread. We discussed in Chapter Two how God's plan is for His glory and the knowledge of His glory to cover the earth. He is so intent on that being true that He spoke this promise through Moses, Isaiah, and Habakkuk. There is no way for God's glory to cover the earth if the move of His Spirit is confined to one location. God desires for revival to spread and impact every area.

We find in our passage from 2 Chronicles that what Josiah did in confronting sin and restoring God's presence in Jerusalem he also did "in the towns" beyond Jerusalem. From the beginning it has been the intent of God for man to cover the earth. To Adam and Eve, God said to *"Be fruitful and increase in number; fill the earth and subdue it" (Genesis 1:28)*. Being created in God's image, we carry His presence – His glory – in our spirits. God desires us to allow His Spirit and glory to be alive in us and to spread throughout the land.

God told Abraham to leave his country and go to a land the Lord would show him. God's intent was to bless Abraham and to bless the world through him. God's desire was to revive Abraham and to see that revival spread through him. God's glory is to cover the earth through men and women who carry His glory. He initially revealed that in and through Abraham, and He is always looking for men and women through who He can continue to reveal His glory.

One of the final things Jesus said to His disciples prior to His ascension to Heaven is this:

But you will receive power when the Holy Spirit comes on you; and you will be my witnesses in Jerusalem, and in all Judea and Samaria, and to the ends of the earth. Acts 1:8

Jesus was telling His disciples that God's plan had not changed. God was going to begin a powerful move of His Spirit in Jerusalem – but it was not to remain there. God desires to spread His message, His power, and His presence throughout the world. Look at this passage of Acts 8 and notice how God accomplished His plan:

And on that day a great persecution began against the church in Jerusalem, and they were all scattered throughout the regions of Judea and Samaria, except the apostles. Some devout men buried Stephen, and made loud lamentation over him. But Saul began ravaging the church, entering house after house, and dragging off men and women, he would put them in prison. Therefore, those who had been scattered went about preaching the word. Acts 8:1-4

Even when persecution and setbacks came to try and stop what God was doing, His Word still spread. God's desire is for revival to work in you and spread through you. If we will allow Him to do so, He can accomplish great things through our lives. Josiah's name can mean fire of God, and we see in our passage that God was spreading His fire to the surrounding areas. "In the towns of Manasseh, Ephraim and Simeon, as far as Naphtali, and in the ruins around them" God's fire spread. Let us consider the significance of the spread of revival as well as the areas to which revival spread.

1. Manasseh

Manasseh means "causing to forget." Manasseh was the first born son of Joseph and was named such as Joseph declared *"It is because God has made me forget all my trouble and all my father's household" (Genesis 41:51).* A large part of revival is erasing your past and giving you a fresh start. I find it significant that the first place revival spread was Manasseh. I hear God saying, "Not only am I pouring out My Spirit, I am also making all things new for my people. No longer will you be held captive by where you have been." Consider the promise recorded by the Prophet Joel:

"Then I will make up to you for the years that the swarming locust has eaten, the creeping locust, the stripping locust and the gnawing locust, My great army which I sent among you. "You will have plenty to eat and be satisfied and praise the name of the LORD your God, Who has dealt wondrously with you; then My people will never be put to shame. "Thus you will know that I am in the midst of Israel, and that I am the LORD your God, and there is no other; and My people will never be put to shame. Joel 2:25-27

God's promise is for the return of what has been stolen and the erasing of what has taken place. By spreading revival to Manasseh, God was once again reminding His people of this truth. The first thing revival is going to do is give you a fresh start. As we allow God's Spirit to work in our lives and erase the past and the effects of the past, we will see fresh opportunities laid out before us.

Oftentimes many of us never progress into our destiny for today because we find ourselves anchored in our yesterday. Whether through the deception of the enemy or the unfriendly statements by others, we can feel trapped and hopeless before God. That is simply not true. By revival spreading to Manasseh first, it was God's way of declaring that He is able to give a fresh start and to wipe the slate clean.

Manasseh screams of salvation. Nobody is a lost cause, nobody is beyond the reach of God. It does not matter where you have been, God sees and knows where He desires to take you. Allow God's Spirit to break the hold of yesterday and bring you into today's destiny.

2. Ephraim

Ephraim means "I shall be doubly fruitful." Joseph's second son he named Ephraim and said, *"It is because God has made me fruitful in the land of my suffering" (Genesis 41:52).* It is significant to note that before Ephraim was Manasseh. It is not possible to be fruitful when your past has you trapped.

Revival increases fruitfulness. As God is working in your life, intimacy and connection between you and Him will increase and cause more fruit to be produced through you. By spreading to Manasseh and clearing the hurdle of the past, revival was able to spread to Ephraim and bring increased fruit. Recall again that Jesus desires for us to bear fruit that lasts (see John 15). This is accomplished in revival. Revival is a blessing for you and in you, and also a blessing through you as it spreads to others.

One thing we cannot afford to forget about fruit, however, is that fruit takes time to develop. Many times in our lives, or in the lives of others, we would like to see things happening more quickly. By action more than words I have often prayed, "God give me patience, but do it now." We are so quick to forget that God's process is perfect, but God's ways and timing are not like our own.

While Manasseh speaks of salvation, Ephraim speaks of a continued walk with the Lord. In the natural, fruit can only be produced when the seed is fertilized and ultimately when the seed dies. By spending time with the Lord, in His presence – in revival, we are allowing the seed of salvation He planted in our hearts to become fertilized by His Spirit. At the same time, we also are allowing our own motives and agendas to die in order that God's fruit may be produced. Consider what the prophet Hosea says concerning Ephraim:

O Ephraim, what more have I to do with idols? It is I who answer and look after you. I am like a luxuriant cypress; from Me comes your fruit. Hosea 14:8

The fruit that is produced comes from God. We must learn to allow the fruit producing process to play out in our own lives and in the lives of those around us. The fruit that we allow to be produced in the right manner will be more tasty and appealing than fruit we may produce in unnatural ways.

It is also significant that after Joseph was reunited with his father Jacob, he brought his two sons, Manasseh and Ephraim, to him to receive a blessing. The custom was for the patriarch (Jacob) to lay his right hand on the oldest or first born son, indicating he was receiving the greater blessing. When Joseph presented his sons to his father, however, Jacob crossed his arms and placed his right hand on the head of Ephraim, giving him the blessing of the first born. When Joseph tried to correct him on this apparent mistake, Jacob said,

But his father refused and said, "I know, my son, I know; he also will become a people and he also will be great. However, his younger brother shall be greater than he, and his descendants shall become a multitude of nations. He blessed them that day, saying, "By you Israel will pronounce blessing, saying, 'May God make you like Ephraim and Manasseh!'" Thus he put Ephraim before Manasseh.
Genesis 48:19-20

When the blessing was bestowed, Ephraim received the double portion or first born blessing. Manasseh is comparable to our experience of salvation, when our past is cleared; Ephraim is comparable to our ongoing relationship with God – a relationship that is fruitful and blessed. God desires that your days of fruitfulness be greater than your past failures. I once told our church that no matter how fruitless your past may have been, God desires your fruitfulness to be even greater through Him. This is a sign of revival spreading in your life as you continue to grow and move forward into greater places of blessing.

One more thing that I feel must be pointed out here is considering the birthright or the first born. In terms of the sons of Jacob, Reuben was the first born and the rightful heir in terms of lineage and importance within the family tree. Consider, however, this statement from 1 Chronicles:

Now the sons of Reuben the firstborn of Israel (for he was the firstborn, but because he defiled his father's bed, his birthright was given to the sons of Joseph the son of Israel; so that he is not enrolled in the genealogy according to the birthright.

97

*Though Judah prevailed over his brothers, and from
him came the leader, yet the birthright belonged to Joseph).*
1 Chronicles 5:1-2

As a result of sin and various circumstances, the right
of the firstborn was taken from Reuben and given instead to
Joseph's sons. And, with what we considered earlier, Jacob
placed Ephraim ahead of Manasseh. So what we find is that
of the tribes of Israel, Ephraim has been moved into the slot or
place of the firstborn. God has placed fruitfulness at the top of
importance. God desires fruitfulness; He desires that we be
fruitful in our relationship with Him and that we be fruitful for
Him because of that relationship. Revival brings emphasis
and importance to fruitfulness.

3. Simeon

Simeon means "heard." Simeon was the second son of
Jacob, and when Leah bore him she declared, *"Because
the LORD heard that I am not loved, he gave me this one too."
So she named him Simeon (Genesis 29:33).* Jacob had
labored seven years to earn Rachel as his wife. At the end of
that time, he was given her older sister Leah instead. From
that time Leah felt unloved by Jacob in comparison to Rachel.
She felt as though she was second class. The birth of Simeon
caused her to declare that God had heard her even in her
perceived lowly condition.

Some reading this may have the feeling that they are
second class or like Leah, they may even feel as though they
are part of a package deal. "I am only around because he
really wanted her." Did Leah ever feel that? Have you ever
felt that? How about the pastor's spouse who is reading this
book? Do you feel that you are only around the church and

the things of God because you are married to the pastor? Trust me when I say this : that is not true..

Revival spreading to Simeon shows us that God is looking to those who feel unloved or forgotten. God is listening to their cries and their disappointment, and He is going to bring revival in their lives. For those that feel forgotten or unimportant take note that God is listening and paying attention to you. God loves to move and pour out His Spirit in places and among people that may feel or appear to be less important.

When Israel was blessing his sons, he said about Simeon, "I will scatter them in Jacob and disperse them in Israel" (Genesis 49:7). As a people they were to become scattered, disconnected, and seemingly forgotten. Yet, when God sent revival during the reign of Josiah, Simeon is specifically mentioned as a place where revival spread. God is listening, God is paying attention, and God sees where you are whether you realize it or not. When revival spreads to Simeon it is God's way of letting us know that the condition you find yourself in or have been in is not necessarily the condition in which God intends for you to stay. God is looking for an opportunity to come and bring His Kingdom to you and bless you.

4. Naphtali

Naphtali means "wrestling." When Rachel saw that she was not bearing any children for Jacob, she gave him her handmaid Bilhah. As Bilhah gave birth to a second son Rachel said, *"With great wrestlings I have wrestled with my sister, and indeed I have prevailed." So she called his name Naphtali." (Genesis 30:8)*. Naphtali represents fruit produced by wrestling with flesh and blood. Rachel had made her barrenness a source of contention and competition. When we make things more about flesh and blood than we do about God, we are going to be unproductive and barren.

Jacob had toiled fourteen years to have Rachel as his wife. His love for her was not based upon what she produced. He simply loved her. She felt, however, that it was necessary to do something in order to gain or maintain Jacob's love. She took it upon herself to wrestle her way to some type of supposed victory. She was wrestling to produce in the natural – Naphtali – what God desired to produce in the supernatural – Joseph. The danger we all face is getting ahead of God, getting in His way, or trying to do His job.

By spreading revival to Naphtali, God was bringing about victory and fruitfulness in the manner in which He intended. God's intent is to bless His people, and for His people to walk in His favor. Choosing to wrestle and fight in our own strength will keep us from receiving God's best. In Deuteronomy, when Moses pronounced a blessing over the tribes, he said this about Naphtali:

Of Naphtali he said, "O Naphtali, satisfied with favor,
And full of the blessing of the LORD, take possession of the
sea and the south." Deuteronomy 33:23

As revival spread to Naphtali, God was making this declared blessing a present reality. It was God bringing man's intentions in line with His own – a picture of revival. I also find it fascinating that God was pouring out his favor and blessing upon that which had been produced by human means. God is able in the midst of revival to even bless and use that which may not have started out in the right manner. God's ability is greater than that of man and He can rewrite and rework any situation for His glory.

5. *In the Ruins*

Ruins means "a place laid waste, ruin, or desolation." God was spreading revival and bringing life where there was no life. This is God's plan for revival. Isaiah prophesied God's intent toward His people's waste places:

Indeed, the LORD will comfort Zion; He will comfort all her waste places. And her wilderness He will make like Eden, and her desert like the garden of the LORD; joy and gladness will be found in her, thanksgiving and sound of a melody.
Isaiah 51:3

It is not God's plan for His people to live in ruin and desolation. Much of the church is living far below where God intends, and often settles for much less than what God has made available. Those who dwelt in the ruins in Josiah's day must have believed they would always dwell in the ruins, but God had other plans. Revival spread to the ruined places as well. There is no situation, circumstance, or people beyond the reach of God. His promise in Isaiah is to bring comfort, fruitfulness and beauty, joy and gladness, thanksgiving and singing to the places in ruin. Revival may have started with Josiah in the palace but it spread to the desolate places; because God is no respecter of persons (Acts 10:34).

Let me reiterate that nobody is beyond the reach of God and nobody is a lost cause. God is not looking for heroes or superstars; He is looking for available people. And He is able to find those available people in the ruins as well as in Jerusalem.

Revival is a fire that cannot be contained but by its very nature must spread. Before we continue, consider this statement used to describe the Azusa Street Revival:

The revival reached out to the rest of the world with a rapidity that is hard to imagine. It was like a fire lit in dry tinder when nobody was looking. It exploded – billowing up and scattering its sparks in every direction. (Cecil Robeck, 2006, p. 187).

God is not finished when He sends revival. His intention is for the fire of revival to spread and reach beyond the borders of its beginning. It can be easy to assume that the move of God is going to begin, live, and remain in Jerusalem, in the midst of where God's people are living. Yet, that is not realistic or desirable in the spiritual so why should it be in the natural?

Perhaps many of you who are reading this book find yourself in that Jerusalem place and with that it may be tough for you to understand what goes with living in the other regions. But for those who are in a Manasseh, Ephraim, Simeon, Naphtali, or a place of ruins, I want you to understand that God wants to reach you and bless you in revival as well.

God is not controlled by boundaries – neither geographical nor circumstantial. As we allow God to move in us and through us, we can see His presence and power spread beyond any human reach.

Back Home (to Jerusalem)

Then he returned to Jerusalem.

Josiah had begun to purge the land in the twelfth year of his reign; here we find him returning to Jerusalem in the eighteenth year of his reign. After seeing revival spread throughout the land for six years, he was compelled to focus on Jerusalem once again. When seeing revival spread to impact the world one must take caution to not lose sight of his own city.

Josiah returned to Jerusalem with a two-fold purpose; to repair the land and to repair the temple. Once again, to purge means to do so physically, ceremonially, and morally. We will discuss the purifying and repairing of the temple, but note that it was also necessary for him to focus on the entire area. It can be very easy to get focused on what God is doing in the church and miss what He wants to do in the community.

My wife and I pastor a church that sits directly across the street from the local high school. While I appreciate the good things God is doing in our church and desire Him to do more, I cannot imagine anything better than seeing the school impacted by God's presence as well. It would be a disappointment to me if a mighty revival came that impacted our church, and even the world, but the local school and community was not impacted. Consider the effects of the 1904 Welsh Revival:

Not only were individual lives changed by the power of the Holy Spirit, but whole communities were changed indeed society itself was changed - Wales was again a God-fearing nation. Public houses became almost empty. Men and women who used to waste their money in getting drunk were now saving it, giving it to help their churches, buying clothes and food for their families. And not only drunkenness, but stealing and other offences grew less and less so that often a magistrate came to court and found there were no cases for him. Men whose language had been filthy before learnt to talk purely. It is related that not only did the colliers put in a better day's work, but also that the pit ponies turned disobedient! The ponies were so used to being cursed and sworn at that they just didn't understand when orders were given in kind, clean words! The dark tunnels underground in the mines echoed with the sounds of prayer and hymns, instead of oaths and nasty jokes and gossip. People who had been careless about paying their bills, or paying back money they had borrowed, paid up all they owed. People who had not been friends for a long time because of something that had happened in the past, forgot their quarrels and were happy together again. In fact, Evan Roberts used to say that there could be no blessing on anyone who had unkind thoughts about anyone else.

Extract taken from Moriah Calvanistic Methodist Website www.moriah.org.uk

Josiah was unwilling to be content with anything less than a powerful impact in his city of reign. He had reign and jurisdiction over the entire nation, but he realized the importance of being stationed in Jerusalem. We find Jesus often returning to His hometown to minister. While He taught that ministry in your hometown is difficult (see Matthew 13:57), He continued to long for effective ministry there.

One of the most important things a church can do to impact their community is to change the mindset or perspective about themselves in the community. Often a church is viewed as focusing on themselves and looking for something from people. Yet Jesus taught the church to be giving. Perhaps the church should apply the famous quote from President John F. Kennedy: "Ask not what your [community] can do for you, ask what you can do for your [community]." It is not realistic to expect the people to beat down the doors of the church. The church must take the message of God to their community. There is too much of the world in the church and not enough of the church in the world.

I am looking for the time when it is said that revival has broken out in entire cities. I imagine a conversation where one says, "I am going to the revival in Carthage, Illinois." His friend replies, "Oh, which church is in revival?" And the greatest answer of all would be, "I hear it does not matter, just as long as you are somewhere in the city limits." Oh God let that become a reality! We must take what God is doing in our lives and in our churches to the world, but not at the neglect of our own neighborhoods. For any pastor reading this, always remember that you do not just pastor a local church in some particular community, but God has also called you to pastor and minister in that community. Let us ever keep taking revival to our communities.

Chapter 7 – Getting God's House in Order

Now in the eighteenth year of his reign, when he had purged the land and the house, he sent Shaphan the son of Azaliah, and Maaseiah an official of the city, and Joah the son of Joahaz the recorder, to repair the house of the LORD his God. They came to Hilkiah the high priest and delivered the money that was brought into the house of God, which the Levites, the doorkeepers, had collected from Manasseh and Ephraim, and from all the remnant of Israel, and from all Judah and Benjamin and the inhabitants of Jerusalem.
2 Chronicles 34:8-9

Repair God's House

He sent Shaphan the son of Azaliah, and Maaseiah an official of the city, and Joah the son of Joahaz the recorder, to repair the house of the LORD his God.

Revival will bring things to order in God's House. In Chapter Five we discussed the removal of the high places, Asherah poles, idols, and altars - all of the wrong ways in which God's people were pursuing Him. We also discussed how Jesus restored the temple in Matthew 21 by bringing back His presence, prayer, praise, and power. A person's house tells a lot about that person, serving as a reflection of who they are. What does God's House say about Him? As Peter says, "it is time for judgment to begin with God's household" (1 Peter 4:17).

Much of what takes place in God's House is a poor reflection on Him. Ask yourself this: Would you allow someone to treat your house the way many treat God's House? I personally cannot imagine being disrespected in my house the way God often is in His. Do we welcome Him and want Him in His House? Have we repossessed His House from Him? All of these questions deserve consideration.

In the book of Revelation, Jesus addressed the seven churches in Asia. Each letter contained His view of them. Many opinions exist about whether each church represents a particular era. I am not going to open that discussion in this book. I do, however, want to consider a few things from the last church addressed – the Church of Laodicea. First off, consider an often quoted verse from that address,

Behold, I stand at the door and knock; if anyone hears My voice and opens the door, I will come in to him and will dine with him, and he with Me. Revelation 3:20

I have heard this quoted during altar times and the calling of sinners to repentance, but this was an address to the church. Jesus is saying that He desires to come in among the church – His House – and fellowship with the people, but He is outside of the church. Is this the picture that most often depicts the House of God today? In His address to the Laodiceans (verses 14-22) Jesus points out some reasons why He is on the outside of the church.

1. The church was lukewarm.

Lukewarm is "a metaphor of the condition of the soul wretchedly fluctuating between a torpor and a fervor of love" (Strong's Concordance). Jesus tells the church He would prefer they either be hot or cold than lukewarm. To be lukewarm means you are not committed to anything, and you blend like a chameleon into whatever situation you find yourself. Jesus is standing outside of the church and knocking because the fire and heat that His presence brings does not mix well with the lukewarm condition.

Obviously, Jesus' preference is that a person be hot instead of lukewarm. But He also says that He would prefer a person be cold than lukewarm. Jesus says it is better to be cold – to know that you are in sin and away from God – than to be lukewarm and have the opinion that all is well. My son likes for me to tell him the story of *Goldilocks and the Three Bears.* In this story, Goldilocks is always looking for that which is just right. She is not interested in the porridge that is too hot or too cold. How many in the church want things just right, and how many churches try to have it just right? Jesus calls us to be hot – on fire – for Him.

Jesus warns that the lukewarm will be spewed or vomited from His mouth. We cannot vomit what is not in our body. So again He is speaking to the church. It is not God's desire for His people to live in a lukewarm state. God desires His people to live in commitment to Him.

Another example would be Ephesus, the first of the seven churches addressed by Jesus in Revelation (see Revelation 2:1-7). Jesus tells them they had left their first love; He pleads with them to *"consider how far [they] have fallen! Repent and do the things you did at first" (Revelation 2:5).* Were they as committed to Christ as they once were? I challenge each one reading this book to take that same inventory. Are you as committed to Christ as you once were? Or, like the church of Ephesus, have you allowed the activities of Christianity to define you? What we do for God should flow out of the relationship we have with Him. We should not define who we are in Christ by what we do for Christ. He then tells the church in Ephesus to get back to doing what keeps the love relationship with God strong. Each of us can start right now in being hot in our Christianity – our relationship with God.

2. The church had misconceptions about their condition.

The church had a perception of their condition as being rich, having acquired wealth, and in need of nothing. God told them, however, *"you do not realize that you are wretched, pitiful, poor, blind and naked" (see Revelation 3:17).* God's Word constantly reminds us that man looks on the outward appearance but God looks on the heart (1 Samuel 16:7). How often do we see ourselves as better than what we really are?

Typically this problem stems from improper perspective. A repairing of the church will help her see herself through the eyes of God. The church is to be the bride of Christ, and His desire is that we view ourselves that way as well and live in a way that matches that view. When the world's standards become the guide of the church, the world's results become the norm for the church. We can put so much emphasis on results and worldly standards that we exert all of our effort and energy pursuing the wrong ideal, a false finish line. Understanding who we are will help to shape who we become.

3. The church was in pursuit of things that were not important.

Jesus counsels the church to buy from Him things that have true eternal value. So much of what the church was and is in pursuit of is temporal and earthly. Whereas Peter was able to say to the lame man at the gate in Acts 3, *"Silver or gold I do not have, but what I do have I give you. In the name of Jesus Christ of Nazareth, walk";* I fear in much of the church today we would be forced to declare the opposite. Listen to these words written by Dr. Michael Brown,

> *We have put our treasures in earthly things. Heaven and hell have become figures of speech. There is hardly any brokenness for the lost. (Do we really believe people without Jesus are lost – forever?) How often have we wept for an unsaved family member or friend? And if our stomach is not our god, why so little fasting for a genuine revival and outpouring? Why so little sacrifice here if eternal life is our real goal?* (Brown, 1993, p. 5).

Jesus said that this church believed they had become rich, had acquired great wealth, and were in need of nothing. The way the Laodicean church saw it they were in a great position. Yet in all their pursuit what did they really have? While on paper it may seem they had gained it all, at what expense was it gained? We need the house of God repaired so that we will again realize what the purpose of our pursuit should be – God's Kingdom and glory.

4. Jesus loves the church.

The main reason that Jesus is standing outside of the church wanting to be let in is because of His great love for the church. When I consider the Godhead it occurs to me that you cannot separate the Father from His glory; you cannot separate Holy Spirit from His power; and you cannot separate Christ from His love. Love is the characteristic that drove Jesus during His life on earth and it continues to drive Him today in His pursuit of you and me.

Often we read about Jesus being moved by compassion and meeting the needs of people. This is Who

He is. In Chapter Five we examined the compassion and love Christ has for His church by exploring His entry into the temple (see Matthew 21). Because He loves the church so much He wants to restore His presence, prayer, praise, and power.

During the revival led by Josiah it was necessary for God's House to be repaired. May God send a revival in our day that would once again repair the House of God.

Paying the Price

They came to Hilkiah the high priest and delivered the money that was brought into the house of God.

Hilkiah was given the money for the repair of the temple. They were not holding back any portion, they were giving everything to see God's House restored and God's presence honored.

There is a price to be paid for seeing an outpouring of God's Spirit. During the days of the Brownsville Revival, Thomas Trask, then the General Superintendent of the Assemblies of God, and Wayde Goodall, executive director of the Enrichment Journal, interviewed Pastor John Kilpatrick and Evangelist Steve Hill (see the issue from Spring 1998). Rev Trask asked about the price of revival and this was the answer given by Pastor Kilpatrick:

During the revival, my responsibility is to carry the dung shovel. I deal with things that nobody else can deal with-the hard cases of people that are rebellious or want to cause problems. With a revival this size, I have to deal with problems almost every night.

People also do not understand the magnitude of the Satanic attack. Because we are under such severe attack, there have

111

been many times when we've had to hold each other and pray intensely for one another before we could go out and start the service. When pastors begin to pray for revival, they need to take all this into consideration. You ask, "Is it worth it?" Thank God, it's worth it. But nothing comes without a price. Revival is not easy sailing. Pastors need to understand that.

While the primary repairs needed in God's House are spiritual, we cannot neglect the physical needs. I believe God's House should be the absolute best it can be. I am not advocating placing all of our attention on buildings; we have already been down that road and we have glorious facilities that are empty of God's presence. I do believe, however, that we should take care of the physical House of God – the church building – in the best way that we can. May we not hold back anything, but pay the price in all ways to see God honored.

Protecting what God is Doing

Which the Levites, the doorkeepers, had collected.

To watch or keep the door or gate meant to guard, protect, or keep safe. It speaks of preserving or keeping watch over something of value. This position of importance was taken on by the Levites or priests. They were the gatekeepers of God's House. In 1 Chronicles 26 we find David leaving Solomon instructions about the installation of gatekeepers when Solomon would complete the building of the temple.

Guard was alongside of guard: There were six Levites a day
on the east, four a day on the north, four a day on the south
and two at a time at the storehouse. As for the court to the
west, there were four at the road and two at the court itself.
1 Chronicles 26:16-18 (NIV)

The responsibility of the gatekeeper was to protect the purity of God's House. As revival is moving and spreading, we too have a distinct responsibility to protect the purity of God's House, thus protecting what God is doing in our midst. It is surprising how quickly things can creep in and thwart a move of God. In his book *Feast of Fire* (Kilpatrick, 1995), Pastor John Kilpatrick addresses this issue with what he refers to as the "Devil's Five Deadly D's." This information is found in Chapter Ten of his book, but I will give a quick synopsis here.

1. Doubt – "Suspicion, doubt and skepticism are all inevitable responses any time the Holy Spirit moves in a congregation in a new or unaccustomed way" (p 111-12).
2. Distractions – There will be people who are distracted by watching someone who is acting fleshly in the midst of a move of God, and therefore discount all that God is doing. There will be others who become distracted by things at home, work, or in life in general.
3. Disappointment – "Many Christians get disappointed that life goes on after revival; they just want to stay in the presence of the Lord feeling blessed, refreshed, and empowered. What we need to recognize is that these times of refreshing come to help prepare us for the natural things of life, not keep us from them" (p 115).

4. Discouragement – "Discouragement will come to all who seek the Lord" (p 116). The issue is coming out of that place of discouragement and not allowing ourselves to wallow in it.
5. Defamation – We must determine if our reputation is more valuable than a move of God. Are you bothered by the thought of being connected to the "weird church?"

When revival is taking place we can rest assured that there will be attacks and challenges that come to try and steal what God is doing. We are the "holy priesthood" (1 Peter 2:9), and we each have the responsibility of keeping the gate. Let us take seriously the responsibility afforded us by God to protect and keep the beautiful things God does in our lives through revival.

As revival spreads and impacts the world beyond where it begins, it does not change our responsibility to continue to be faithful in the promotion of God in our own city. Just as Josiah went back to Jerusalem to repair God's House, so we must at all times see that we do not lose our city in an attempt to win the world. Are we willing to pay the price and guard what God is doing? Are we willing to allow God to be God in all His fullness and power? The only limitations to what God can do are the ones we place on Him. The Bible, as well as other books written about revival, is not just a compilation of stories of things God *can do*; it shows us what God *wants to do* in our lives and in our day. I say, Lord, revive us once again!

Chapter 8 – When God Trusts You

Then they gave it into the hands of the workmen who had the oversight of the house of the LORD, and the workmen who were working in the house of the LORD used it to restore and repair the house. They in turn gave it to the carpenters and to the builders to buy quarried stone and timber for couplings and to make beams for the houses which the kings of Judah had let go to ruin. The men did the work faithfully with foremen over them to supervise: Jahath and Obadiah, the Levites of the sons of Merari, Zechariah and Meshullam of the sons of the Kohathites, and the Levites, all who were skillful with musical instruments. 2 Chronicles 34:10-12

A Mutual Trust

Then they entrusted it to the men appointed to supervise the work on the LORD's temple. (NIV)

In Chapter One I shared about my ongoing experience with learning to trust God. This is such an important part of revival. God has called us to trust Him with our heart and not with our own understanding (Proverb 3:5-6). As we grow in our trust in and of Him, He is able to do more in and through our lives. I have personally been overwhelmed over the last several months of my life as I have grown in my own ability to trust God. I would love to say I have it mastered, but it is an ongoing journey. Most things with God are more about the journey than the destination, and learning to trust Him is no different.

I continue to learn that trust with God is not a one-way street. Just as He calls us to trust Him, we need to realize that He wants to trust us as well. From the beginning, God's intent has been to empower man with responsibility. At creation

God's intention in creating man was for him to rule over the earth. God was putting trust in man's ability to fulfill his purpose. When Adam and Eve committed sin by eating of the tree of the knowledge of good and evil, that trust relationship was damaged. God did not suddenly become untrustworthy – man did. Even still God did not give up His desire to trust you and me. .

Jesus came to earth to renew this trust relationship. During His mission, Jesus constantly told His disciples that a time was coming when He would be leaving the earth. He said it was good for them that He was going away, so He could send Holy Spirit to help them and empower them to fulfill His plan. With the coming of God's Holy Spirit, the trust relationship was strengthened. As Jesus told His disciples, *"the Spirit of Truth . . . lives with you and will be in you" (John 14:17)*. In the Garden, God was *with man*; now God by His Spirit would be both *with* and *in man*. God desires to do things both in and through our lives, to entrust and to empower us with the furtherance of His Kingdom. Can God trust you?

Look at what the Psalmist says about David:

Once you spoke in a vision, to your faithful people you said: "I have bestowed strength on a warrior; I have raised up a young man from among the people. I have found David my servant; with my sacred oil I have anointed him. My hand will sustain him; surely my arm will strengthen him. The enemy will not get the better of him; the wicked will not oppress him. I will crush his foes before him and strike down his adversaries. My faithful love will be with him, and through my name his horn will be exalted. Psalm 89:19-24 (NIV)

We find here God's desire is to trust and to bless. When God finds one He can trust, He pours out His blessing and His favor upon him. Look at what God promised to David, and promises to the one he finds trustworthy:

1. God bestows strength upon him as a warrior.

God found David and bestowed His own strength upon him. God called David a warrior. I am again reminded of 2 Chronicles 16:9 where the Lord promises to "show Himself strong" on behalf of one He finds committed to Him. When God finds you trustworthy, He shows His strength in and through your life. Throughout his life David was known as a warrior. When his son Solomon was preparing to build the temple of God, he declared about his father David,

"You know that because of the wars waged against my father David from all sides, he could not build a temple for the Name of the LORD his God until the LORD put his enemies under his feet. But now the LORD my God has given me rest on every side, and there is no adversary or disaster." 1 Kings 5:3-4

David was the one that God used as a warrior to bring victory to His people. God truly delights to show Himself strong for His people. When He found David to be trustworthy and ready, He worked through his life as a mighty warrior.

We do not serve a weak God. Our God is not limited in His strength or ability. All things are under His authority and control. When we allow Him to be Who He really is in our lives, we find His strength at work on our behalf. God is looking to strengthen warriors for His Kingdom once again.

2. *God raises him up from his youth.*

God had looked beyond the outward appearance and man's perceived shortcomings and found in David a heart with which He could work. When God finds you trustworthy He is able to raise you up to the place He desires you to be. It is difficult for God to find one like this because many spend so much time trying to raise themselves up into a position of greatness. We need not fear being great in the Lord, but we also need not make that our motivation or agenda. There is a big difference between being raised up by God and making it your mission to climb to where you want to be for God. God desires to raise you up to where He desires you to be.

So many people are waiting for a chosen person to do something special. If God finds you faithful and trustworthy, He will raise you up and use you mightily for the advancement of His Kingdom. David did not hide from what God had planned for him. He made himself fully available and therefore God used him fully.

And as we considered in Chapter One, age is not a factor. Josiah took the throne at the age of eight. God raised up David from his youth. Jesus amazed the religious leaders in the temple at the age of twelve (see Luke 2:47). Age is just a number and not a representation of ability or usefulness. God is looking for people of all ages whom He can raise up, with His presence and Spirit, to see great things accomplished for His Kingdom.

3. *God anoints him.*

Man appoints but God anoints. Man would have chosen one of Jesse's other sons who gave the appearance of being much more qualified for leading a nation. But God had anointed David. Your anointing and your gifting will make room for you as you prove yourself to be trustworthy to God. God says He anointed David because he found him as His servant. David had proven himself faithful in all ways and God trusted him to handle the anointing.

So Samuel took the horn of oil and anointed him in the presence of his brothers, and from that day on the Spirit of the LORD came upon David in power. 1 Samuel 16:13

God's anointing is not to be taken lightly or for granted. The Spirit of the Lord came powerfully upon David from the moment he was anointed by Samuel. God's design is for His anointing to come upon those He finds trustworthy, to empower them to do great things for Him. We need not cower or hide from the anointing that God places on our lives. His anointing empowers us to do what His purpose has employed us to do. No one should try to walk in God's service without having His anointing applied. The anointing is not for you, however, to exalt you or to make you shine. His anointing is for His Kingdom, so that through one who is anointed He can be glorified and others may receive ministry from Him. May each of us allow God's anointing to work in, on, and through our lives to bring about His purpose. At the beginning of His earthly ministry Jesus declared:

"The Spirit of the Lord is on me, because he has anointed me to preach good news to the poor. He has sent me to proclaim freedom for the prisoners and recovery of sight for the blind, to release the oppressed, to proclaim the year of the Lord's favor." Luke 4:18-19

God's anointing – God's Hand – is upon you with a purpose. We have a responsibility to effectively fulfill that purpose by walking in His anointing to bring good news, freedom, and the favor of the Lord to our world.

4. God's Hand sustains him and His arm strengthens him.

When God shows Himself strong on someone's behalf, it is an ongoing relationship. When God finds you trustworthy, He sets you up to succeed in Him. God uses the same amount of strength to sustain you as He did to raise you up to the place He designed for you. The only time we are in danger of losing our place is when we make it about our own hands and strength and not about God.

Isaiah 40:12 declares *"Who has measured the waters in the hollow of his hand, or with the breadth of his hand marked off the heavens?"* God's hands are big. I remember singing in Children's Church, "He's got the whole world in His hands." If we believe that God's Hand is big enough to hold the universe, then we should never question if it is big enough to hold us. God will sustain you and uphold you. About His righteous, God declares *"though he may stumble, he will not fall, for the LORD upholds him with his hand" (Psalm 37:24)*. The Lord is willing and able to keep you.

5. God fights against his enemies.

Psalm 89 tells us that the enemy will not get the better of us or oppress us. God will crush our foes and strike down our adversaries. What a wonderful promise! This strengthens the Psalmist to say,

The LORD is with me; I will not be afraid.
What can man do to me? The LORD is with me; he is my
helper. I will look in triumph on my enemies. Psalm 118:6-7

There are times when the thought of making ourselves fully available to God is frightening. There are times when we become concerned about the enemy of our souls and the opposition he is sure to provide as we actively serve God. But I challenge you to find one person in the Bible that became available to God and truly suffered defeat at the hands of the enemy. We could talk about many who faced battles and challenges of great difficulty. Job, for example, was tested unlike anyone else, but he did not lose. Paul, who suffered great persecution and challenges, said this:

Therefore we do not lose heart. Though outwardly we are
wasting away, yet inwardly we are being renewed day by
day. For our light and momentary troubles are achieving for us
an eternal glory that far outweighs them all. So we fix our eyes
not on what is seen, but on what is unseen. For what is seen
is temporary, but what is unseen is eternal.
2 Corinthians 4:16-18

The underlying issue here is perspective. If we go into battle with a mindset of defeat, we will come out of the battle defeated. If we are focusing on the enemy and the attacks he brings, then we put ourselves in a position of defeat. But if we maintain our focus on Christ and the strength He provides for us, regardless of what comes our way, we will stand strong and march forward in the Lord, accomplishing great things for Him. The Lord delights to fight on behalf of His own!

6. God's faithful love will be with him.

Who could ask for anything more? In the midst of God moving in our life, there may be times of loneliness, isolation, and the onset of discouragement. We, however, have the promise that God's love will be with us. Even in the weakest of times, God's love is able to bring us strength. God's love is more powerful than the mightiest of armies or weapons. Keep this powerful truth from Romans ever before you:

For I am convinced that neither death nor life, neither angels nor demons, neither the present nor the future, nor any powers, neither height nor depth, nor anything else in all creation, will be able to separate us from the love of God that is in Christ Jesus our Lord. Romans 8:38-39

The love of God will be with us, in and through all things, and nothing shall separate us from His love. God desires to bless, use, and empower us for great things. And He promises to be with us at all times, ever strengthening us with His love.

Can God find us trustworthy and show Himself strong on our behalf? Can God trust us with His presence, His anointing, His revival? He desires to do so. As we learn to trust Him we also must learn the value of proving ourselves trustworthy to Him. As He finds us trustworthy and faithful, He will do great things in and through our lives.

Expanding the Trust – Delegation

Then they gave it into the hands of the workmen who had the oversight of the house of the LORD, and the workmen who were working in the house of the LORD used it to restore and repair the house. They in turn gave it to the carpenters and to the builders to buy quarried stone and timber for couplings and to make beams for the houses which the kings of Judah had let go to ruin.

There was far too much to be done for Josiah to take care of it himself. The need for delegating responsibility was obvious. Imagine the burn out or lack of progress had Josiah attempted to do everything himself. The work on the temple was carried out by those appointed and capable. There was oversight and supervision, but the work was distributed and delegated.

As Moses was leading the children of Israel, he was becoming overtaxed and on the verge of burn out as a result. If it had not been for his father-in-law Jethro's suggesting he delegate some responsibility, the story of the Israelites might have turned out much differently. Listen to Jethro's warning:

Moses' father-in-law replied, "What you are doing is not good. You and these people who come to you will only wear yourselves out. The work is too heavy for you; you cannot handle it alone. Listen now to me and I will give you some advice, and may God be with you. You must be the people's representative before God and bring their disputes to him. Teach them the decrees and laws, and show them the way to live and the duties they are to perform. But select capable men from all the people—men who fear God, trustworthy men who hate dishonest gain—and appoint them as officials over thousands, hundreds, fifties and tens. Have them serve as judges for the people at all times, but have them bring every difficult case to you; the simple cases they can decide themselves. That will make your load lighter, because they will share it with you. If you do this and God so commands, you will be able to stand the strain, and all these people will go home satisfied." Exodus 18:17-23

Moses was wearing himself out by trying to take care of everyone and everything in the camp. God never intends for anyone to become overtaxed in their work for Him. He never puts anyone in a position of isolation, without others around that can be of benefit to them. If you are in a leadership position in ministry and you are feeling burned out, take a look around you and recognize those God has put there to help carry the load.

Often the reason people struggle with delegating is the feeling of being the only one truly qualified to get something done right. Rather than have someone else do it, they choose to do it themselves. Not only is that tiring and ultimately non-productive, it is also a sign of pride. Typically those who cannot release responsibility into the care of others also struggle with releasing their cares into the hands of God. God wants to work on that in your life. Revival affords a great opportunity to see new leaders raised up in the Lord, and God wants to use you to help in that process. We need to be careful that we do not assume too much ownership and control over what God has entrusted to us.

And when you do delegate responsibility, do so in a trusting way. If you give someone the responsibility to do something, make sure they also have the authority.

Moses listened to his father-in-law and did everything he said. He chose capable men from all Israel and made them leaders of the people, officials over thousands, hundreds, fifties and tens. They served as judges for the people at all times. The difficult cases they brought to Moses, but the simple ones they decided themselves. Exodus 18:24-26

Give Honor Where it is Due

These men paid the workers who repaired and restored the temple. (NIV)

Not giving someone the authority along with the responsibility will only cause frustration and unwillingness to continue. Many in the church have given up serving opportunities because of this incorrect approach toward delegation. In the same vein, it is imperative that when we delegate, and when people serve, we give honor to whom honor is due (see Romans 13:7). Those who did the work of repairing and restoring the temple were paid. Their work was noticed and rewarded. Things should never be different in the church. But think about how many thankless deeds you yourself have performed. This is a valuable key in sustaining revival. People deserve to be shown appreciation.

I am not just referring to salary. Not all churches can afford to pay everyone who serves. There is not a church on the planet, however, that does not have the ability to show appreciation in any number of ways. As a pastor I have found that one of the quickest ways to discourage a person is to make them feel unappreciated and unnoticed. I have been guilty of that. God help me to learn and apply this important element of honor. What gets appreciated gets completed. If you fail to thank someone for what they do, the next time you need something done they may fail to do it. I realize some reading this may not want any sign of appreciation and to you I say I do not care. The person showing the appreciation needs to do so more than you may need to receive it. It is an important life principle.

When you are the one on the receiving end of honor or thanks, make sure you learn to graciously receive what is given to you. A simple approach is to say thank you and tell them it was nice of them to say. It is not pride to receive appreciation, but it is often false humility to deny the appreciation.

The Work Was Done

The men did the work faithfully.

In the Enrichment Journal interview of Pastor Kilpatrick and Evangelist Hill I referred to in Chapter Six, Rev. Trask asked what they had learned about revival. Here is the answer given by Steve Hill:

We're in our third year, and crowds continue to swarm this place. We have learned that revival is very hard work. Anyone praying for revival needs to be prepared. I compare it to war. It's like training for battle, and when battle breaks out, there's absolutely no rest. People ask us all the time, "How are you doing?" We're doing fine - as well as anybody can be doing after almost 3 years of revival. It's grueling hard work. God never puts revival on the sale table. It'll cost you everything.

When it comes to a move of God there is nothing easy. There is work to be done. Church life becomes intensified, your responsibilities increase, and the pace in general becomes quicker. It can be challenging and exhausting, but it is worth it. It is nice to think that when revival breaks out things will instantly become easier; but that is simply not true. What does happen is that you have a deeper sense of God's grace and power at work in your life to enable you to do the work required.

When these men were entrusted with the work of repairing the temple, they went at it full force. *The workers labored faithfully.* When God is moving in our lives, and we know there is work to be done, the only way to approach it is faithfully and with fervor. They worked with determination and steadfastness.

For work to be completed faithfully it takes focus and commitment. If at any point we get distracted and get off course, we are left with many incomplete projects. When God has given you a job to do, the only way to approach it is to labor faithfully and get the task done. As we saw earlier in this chapter, God will strengthen you and help you to be effective as you are trustworthy and faithful.

I want God to find me trustworthy and faithful so that He may show Himself strong on my behalf. As I am learning to trust God more, I am also learning to make myself trustworthy to Him. He has held nothing back from me, so I have no reason to hold anything back from Him. As I commit to stepping out and doing what He has created and called me to do, I also know I cannot do it alone. I need you and you need me. There is much work to be done for God's Kingdom, and together we can accomplish much. Let us faithfully be about the Father's business. Neither God nor the world is looking for a spiritual hero. But both need someone to be available for and surrendered to His anointing. Is that someone you?

Chapter 9 – Pastoring Revival

The men did the work faithfully with foremen over them to supervise: Jahath and Obadiah, the Levites of the sons of Merari, Zechariah and Meshullam of the sons of the Kohathites, and the Levites, all who were skillful with musical instruments. They were also over the burden bearers, and supervised all the workmen from job to job; and some of the Levites were scribes and officials and gatekeepers.
2 Chronicles 34:12-13

Revival Must be Pastored

Over them to supervise: Jahath and Obadiah, the Levites of the sons of Merari, Zechariah and Meshullam of the sons of the Kohathites,

Direction and oversight were in place as the work of the ministry and the spread of revival were taking place. Notice they were there to direct. They were not there to control, but to guide. There can be a fine line between controlling what God is doing and pastoring or directing what God is doing.

As a pastor it can be so easy to hold tightly to the reins of ministry, and therefore not allow God to do what He wants to do. One of the easiest things to learn is how to do church and ministry without God. I can personally attest to that. I can recall and recount moments when my actions and decisions were basically saying I knew better than God what needed to be done in and for the church. This is a slippery slope and can lead us to a place we do not want to find ourselves.

One of the easiest things to do is to step into a familiar place of anointing, something we spoke about in Chapter Eight. It is easy to find yourself in a situation that seems similar to something you have experienced before, and you can convince yourself that in the anointing you know what to do. The challenge as a pastor, however, is to recognize that while God is consistent He is not guaranteed to always do things the same. Learning to follow His guidance is much more important than knowing how to do things.

The value of this portion of our foundational passage is realizing that with everything that was going on, the revival was carried along by effective pastoral oversight. Pastor, when God brings revival to your life, your church, and your city, there are some key characteristics from this passage we need to exemplify. Remember that to whom much is given, much is required (Luke 12:48); when God finds you trustworthy and pours out His Spirit in and on your life, He will be looking to you to pastor and lead what He has begun and what He will continue to do.

I want to consider the names of the leaders mentioned to draw some insight into the characteristics and qualities of those who were directing or pastoring the work of God. Also, I want to point out that there was a team of directors in place. Call to mind our discussion in Chapter Eight about delegation, and realize that God is not looking for or expecting you to do it alone, and the church does not benefit from a one man show. If you do not see in yourself some of these characteristics and qualities, do not be afraid to surround yourself with others that can provide them.

Jahath

Jahath means he will snatch up, and it speaks of attention, focus, and quick action. It speaks of the much needed gift of discernment. How vitally important it is for those leading and directing a revival to have discernment.

From a natural standpoint, discernment can be defined as the ability to judge well. It speaks of right perception and right response to that perception. For some it is built in like intuition; for others it does not come as easily.

From a biblical standpoint, discernment is listed as one of the nine gifts of the Holy Spirit as described in 1 Corinthians 12. The discerning of spirits enables you to recognize and distinguish between spirits that are operating, whether the source is human, demonic, or divine. This gift manifests when a person is given insight by the Holy Spirit to recognize the activity and motive of a spirit that is at work. We must be careful to not confuse discerning of spirits with being critical, as there is a huge difference. There are some that are critical of anything and everything they do not understand, yet call it discernment.

Within the context of revival, this gift or quality can prove extremely important and beneficial. In some instances it can be the key to protecting and sustaining what God is doing. You can rest assured that when God's Spirit is moving, there will be elements of the flesh and the demonic that will try to interrupt or steal the spotlight. Discernment is important for protecting God's people from things that are false.

A great biblical example is found in Acts 16. While ministering in Philippi, Paul and Silas were seeing God do wonderful things. There was a spirit at work in that region that began to interfere. Look at what the Scripture says:

Once when we were going to the place of prayer, we were met by a slave girl who had a spirit by which she predicted the future. She earned a great deal of money for her owners by fortune-telling. This girl followed Paul and the rest of us, shouting, "These men are servants of the Most High God, who

are telling you the way to be saved." She kept this up for m[
days. Finally Paul became so troubled that he turned aroun[
and said to the spirit, "In the name of Jesus Christ I comman[
you to come out of her!" At that moment the spirit left her.
Acts 16:16-18 (NIV)

God was moving in the area and the enemy was getting annoyed and decided to get involved. Through this woman, the enemy was working to interfere with and even try to stop what God was doing. The lady "followed Paul and the rest" for days, and she continuously shouted, *"These men are servants of the Most High God, who are telling you the way to be saved."* The spirit in her was working to align itself with what God was doing through Paul and Silas, and from an outside perspective it appeared that she was part of the ministry team. We also see that this woman had earned a great deal of money for her owners through the power of the spirit at work in her. When Paul and Silas came and preached Jesus, and through them God's Spirit moved, the spirit in this woman became very territorial. The enemy does not want to give up territory he believes he owns.

Imagine if Paul had said nothing and allowed this to continue. The people in Philippi would have naturally assumed that this woman was part of their ministry team, and they would have believed that the same spirit was at work in all of them. Without both the ability to discern and the willingness to exercise that discernment, confusion would have come and remained and God's Spirit would have been misrepresented and not as free to move among the people. Had Paul not confronted this spirit it is unlikely he and Silas would have been put into prison. And if they had not been in prison they would not have been given the opportunity to ne jailer and see his entire family accept Christ

by choosing not to confront false spirits when they are ark, you are choosing to accept them. Discernment is so ucial. We are encouraged by Paul to "covet earnestly the best gifts" (1 Corinthians 12:31), and I find myself coveting discernment. God help all of us to be discerning, and to surround ourselves with those who are discerning, so that we can properly direct and pastor what God is doing in our lives.

Obadiah

Obadiah means servant of Jehovah. To effectively pastor and direct a move of God one must be a servant. No matter what happens in our lives, no matter what God does through our lives or ministries, we must always remember that we are but servants. We are imperfect people with the distinct privilege of serving a perfect God. When our God came to earth as a man, He embodied a servant and humbled Himself to the lowest place (see Philippians 2:5-11). One thing that I keep on the bookshelf in my office is the towel I received when I was licensed to preach with the Assemblies of God. On that white towel, written in gold letters, it says, "*Serve . . . Mark 10:45.*" Jesus did not come to be served, but to serve and He has called for us to follow His example.

The church needs humble servants, and revival will flow through humble servants. Pride and a self-seeking attitude can get in the way of a move of God very quickly. Just before Paul described the attitude of Christ in Philippians 2:5-11, he said this:

Do nothing from selfishness or empty conceit, but with humility of mind regard one another as more important than

*yourselves; do not merely look out for your own persona[l]
interests, but also for the interests of others. Philippians 2:3[.]*

This is the attitude and position of an effective leade[r]
for God. Throughout the Bible the example has been set – to
lead by serving. I used to work in retail before I became full-
time in ministry. At one point I was the acting store manager
of a shoe store. My policy with the staff was this: I would not
ask them to do anything that I was not willing to do myself. I
also told them that if they questioned this policy to call me on
it. One day I asked someone to vacuum the floor. He said he
had never seen me do that job, and he was right. At that
moment I stopped my paperwork, got out the vacuum, and
went to work. My co-worker quickly insisted I turn the
vacuuming duties over to him. He just wanted to see if I was
serious and he quickly found that I was. After that he became
my greatest asset. Leadership is done by example and the
greatest example we can ever hope to set is by serving.

Zechariah

Zechariah means Jehovah remembers. This speaks of
trusting God for the fulfillment of His promises. If you are
going to lead a revival you must trust God to do what He said
He would do. We have touched on trust many times already
throughout this book, and I will not revisit those things again
here. I will say, however, that if God has placed something in
your heart, do not dare back down from that promise. A wise
minister once told me that if God enables you to see it, He will
empower you to do it. It is vitally important to be steadfast and
enduring if you are going to direct and pastor a move of God.
Along the way there are going to be bumps in the road that will
try and discourage you and get you off course. Yet we must
hold on to what God has placed in our hearts and believe that

...iat, He is able to do what He said He would do. ...omises are yes and amen (2 Corinthians 1:20).

...lam

Meshullam means friend. As a pastor we have to make ...ure that we never become too busy or too important for people. We must always be friendly and make sure the people feel as though they are important to us.

In a revival it is easy to become busy and distracted by things that appear more important than people; but everything we do should always come back to people and our ability to connect with them. One of the things that meant so much to me during my time at the Brownsville Revival was how friendly and approachable Pastor John Kilpatrick always seemed. I never personally made contact with him or got to know him, yet I never felt as though I could not have done so. His son told a group of Brownsville students that during each service his dad could tell who was not in attendance by scanning the sanctuary. He had such a shepherd's heart and was so connected to his flock that he was able to recognize the missing sheep, even with the thousands who were in attendance.

Jesus also showed us the importance of always being connected to people. We find an example of this truth in Mark 10 where Jesus healed Bartimaeus from blindness. The moments leading up to the encounter between Jesus and Bartimaues give us insight into how He embodied this characteristic. Mark records this,

They were on their way up to Jerusalem, with Jesus leading the way, and the disciples were astonished, while those who followed were afraid. Mark 10:32 (NIV)

134

Jesus and His disciples were on their way to Jerusalem, where Jesus knew He was going to be beaten and crucified. He had a purpose and was on a mission. He was so focused on the task at hand that Mark records that those who were with him were astonished and afraid. His resolve and focus was something to behold. Jesus was on His way to fulfilling His destiny and it appeared as though nothing was going to stop Him. In verse 46, however, we are introduced to Bartimaeus, who was sitting by the roadside begging. When Bartimaeus learned that Jesus was passing by, he began to cry out to Him for mercy. Many around tried to get him to quiet down and let Jesus pass. It was obvious to everyone that Jesus was on a mission. But something fascinating took place:

Jesus stopped and said, "Call him." Mark 10:49 (NIV)

Even with the focus and determination that was driving Jesus toward Jerusalem, He was still willing to stop and minister to Bartimaeus. Jesus never let His own destiny keep Him from being a friend to people. Can you say the same about yourself? Can I say the same about myself? God help us to be friendly and approachable, and to ensure that people always believe themselves to be important to us. Let us not lose sight of humanity in the midst of our destiny.

The Value of Worship

And the Levites, all who were skillful with musical instruments. They were also over the burden bearers, and supervised all the workmen from job to job; and some of the Levites were scribes and officials and gatekeepers.

Worship is not just about music and the playing of instruments; however, it does have importance throughout

135

Scripture and throughout church history. I find it interesting that those skilled in music *"had charge of the laborers and supervised all the workers from job to job"* (2 Chronicles 34:13). In this I see the value of worship. The moment we cease to worship may be the moment God ceases to act.

Worship at its core is about the condition and posture of our hearts; worship is a lifestyle. God is good and worthy of worship all the time. An emphasis on who God is and a celebration of His glory opens the heavens for His presence to come and do what only God can do. When our praise ascends, God's presence descends. And this is a good place in which to find ourselves.

Before we move on, let us consider the healing of the ten lepers in terms of worship.

And as he entered into a certain village, there met him ten men that were lepers, which stood afar off: And they lifted up their voices, and said, Jesus, Master, have mercy on us. And when he saw them, he said unto them, Go shew yourselves unto the priests. And it came to pass, that, as they went, they were cleansed. And one of them, when he saw that he was healed, turned back, and with a loud voice glorified God, And fell down on his face at his feet, giving him thanks: and he was a Samaritan. And Jesus answering said, Were there not ten cleansed? but where are the nine? There are not found that returned to give glory to God, save this stranger. And he said unto him, Arise, go thy way: thy faith hath made thee whole.
Luke 17:12-19 (KJV)

All ten of the lepers were cleansed which means they were cured or made clean of their disease. But the one who came back to praise was made whole. This means he was saved or rescued from danger or destruction. It denotes salvation in the technical, biblical sense. In response to his praise and worship, this leper received the fullness of God's blessing. I do not want to miss anything God has for me; therefore, I want to live a life of praise and worship unto Him.

There are characteristics and qualities that are essential to be found in those entrusted by God to lead revival. Discernment, service, trust, and friendliness must be genuine ingredients in the leading of a move of God. And these things must pave the way for worship and establish its importance. In this way God will be honored, glorified, and welcomed.

Chapter 10 – Doing Your Part for God

When they were bringing out the money which had been brought into the house of the LORD, Hilkiah the priest found the book of the law of the LORD given by Moses. Hilkiah responded and said to Shaphan the scribe, "I have found the book of the law in the house of the LORD." And Hilkiah gave the book to Shaphan. Then Shaphan brought the book to the king and reported further word to the king, saying, "Everything that was entrusted to your servants they are doing."
2 Chronicles 34:14-16

Using Your Gifts

Some of the Levites were scribes and officials and gatekeepers.

Everyone has something they can contribute to the furtherance of God's Kingdom. In Chapters Seven and Eight we touched on the amount of work that comes with revival as well as the importance of delegation and teamwork. There is plenty to do and you have plenty to offer in seeing the work accomplished. God makes things on purpose and with a purpose – you and I are no different. Each of us is made in a unique way and can be effective for God's Kingdom. Ephesians 2:10 tells us that we are *his workmanship, created in Christ Jesus unto good works, which God hath before ordained that we should walk in them.* God has specifically made you for the purpose of glorifying Him and helping to see His Kingdom advanced.

There are many people who sit in churches week after week feeling as if they have nothing to offer. That is not true. Each person needs to find a way in which he can effectively be used by God, and each church needs to help facilitate the process.

As each one has received a special gift, employ it in serving one another as good stewards of the manifold grace of God.
1 Peter 4:10

It is my belief that each gift should be represented in every local church. Often the reason they are not always represented is that people are afraid to exercise their gifts. I will tell you what I tell our church concerning operating in the gifts: Do not be afraid to make a mistake. It is better to make a mistake as you step out in faith, as opposed to doing nothing because of fear. I would rather someone make a mistake attempting something for God than to get everything right doing nothing. God is not looking for you to be a hero; He just needs an available vessel. God has gifted you in ways that are unique and He desires to utilize you and your gifts in ways that He cannot do through others.

Often when talking to people I am amazed by the gifts, passions, and interests they are hiding. While there are some passions that need to be repented of and broken away from, there are many things that are both acceptable and useful to God. When you serve in an area in which you are passionate, it adds a deeper sense of meaning and fulfillment to your service. It is so important that we learn to utilize our passions for the good of God's Kingdom.

On a practical note, it is also important to know that for which you *are not* passionate. If you are uncomfortable around babies, then do not sign up for the nursery. If you get irritated by teenagers, then being a youth pastor or youth sponsor may not be for you. But if you are drawn to children, and they to you, then find a way to serve in children's ministry,

Sunday School, or some similar capacity. Please communicate your passions, as pastors are not always able to read your mind.

Let your service flow out of who you are. God does not change His mind about using you based on your personality. He does not wish He had made you differently. There is not a cookie cutter mold for servants of God. We are not robots, we are individuals who are *"fearfully and wonderfully made"* (Psalm 139:14).

A youth pastor who served with me had previously been the interim pastor during a time of pastoral transition. He told me that the experience made him believe that he was not cut out to be a pastor, because he believed he could not fit the mold of a pastor. Like many, there was an image in his mind of how a pastor was supposed to appear. We had many conversations about how God had made him as he was, and how God wanted him to serve out of his own personality. I can still remember the day when he told me that he felt God wanted him to be a senior pastor. While I knew that meant I would be losing a very valuable asset, I was so excited for him. I had watched him come so far in his understanding of who he was in Christ, and how to be comfortable in and serve out of that place. He has been effectively serving as a senior pastor for many years now. The ministry he is leading totally fits him and his personality, which is exactly as it should be.

God is also able to use what you have been through to minister to those who are going through similar issues. There is a mutual understanding that comes in these instances. I remember praying with a gentleman at the altar who began to tell me about being in the midst of a difficult divorce. I was not able to completely relate, as I had personally never been in that situation. I knew, however, that one of the other men in our church had been through a similar situation. By connecting these two men it opened a door for ministry that before was not there.

As a pastor I find that my preaching is impacted by my experiences in life. There are things I am able to speak about with more authority because I have been through them. My wife and I struggled for seven years to have a child. The emotions and disappointments we experienced during that time were unbelievable. But that experience has given an avenue for ministry that before then we did not have. We can relate with those in a similar situation. Not only are we able to sympathize but we are able to empathize as well. When you are able to tell someone you have been there, it changes everything. Do not hide from where you have been. God is able to use the experiences from your life to reach and serve others.

Revival will grow and continue as we make ourselves available in service to God and to others. The body of Christ is most effective when each member is doing its part (see 1 Corinthians 12). Let us be guided by this truth:

Now there are varieties of gifts, but the same Spirit. And there are varieties of ministries, and the same Lord. There are varieties of effects, but the same God who works all things in all persons. But to each one is given the manifestation of the Spirit for the common good. 1 Corinthians 12:4-7

Emphasizing God's Word

Hilkiah the priest found the book of the law of the LORD given by Moses. the LORD that had been given through Moses.

When Hilkiah found the Book of the Law, they were reminded of God's original plan, and they saw how far the nation had strayed from God's commands. From the time that the Book of the Law was written, God's intention was as follows:

So Moses wrote this law and gave it to the priests, the sons of Levi who carried the ark of the covenant of the LORD, and to all the elders of Israel. Then Moses commanded them, saying, "At the end of every seven years, at the time of the year of remission of debts, at the Feast of Booths, when all Israel comes to appear before the LORD your God at the place which He will choose, you shall read this law in front of all Israel in their hearing. Assemble the people, the men and the women and children and the alien who is in your town, so that they may hear and learn and fear the LORD your God, and be careful to observe all the words of this law. Their children, who have not known, will hear and learn to fear the LORD your God, as long as you live on the land which you are about to cross the Jordan to possess." Deuteronomy 31:9-13

God's design was that at least every seven years this Book be read in the hearing of the people. God had given a four-part purpose for the reading of His law.

1. *That the people would hear what God said.*

The book of Romans tells us that faith comes by hearing God's Word (10:17). God has always desired for us to hear what He says. When the book was delivered and read to King Josiah, he "rent his clothes" (2 Chronicles 34:19). By hearing God's Word, he realized all the ways in which the nation he was leading had disobeyed God. God has guidelines for living that we can never know or understand if we do not hear them from His word.

2. *That the people would learn from what God said.*

We must be teachable students of God's Word. God's Word has been written for our instruction, and to help us understand Him and to grow in His grace and purpose. Paul says this in the book of Romans:

What shall we say then? Is the Law sin? May it never be! On the contrary, I would not have come to know sin except through the Law; for I would not have known about coveting if the Law had not said, "You shall not covet." Romans 7:7

God's law gives us information for effective living, but we learn not by reading the Word for information, but by reading God's Word for formation. We learn by application – by allowing God's Word to shape our lives. The intent of the Bible is not to ruin a person's life, but rather it is to enhance and to bless a person's life.

3. *That the people would fear the Lord.*

The fear of the Lord carries a bad connotation for some. God has not called us to be afraid of Him. Instead, God's plan is for us to reverence and to respect Him, thus leading us to relationship, service, and obedience. In Exodus 19 and 20 we find the account of God coming down on the mountain, in the presence of all of Israel, to speak to Moses and the people. The people became fearful of God's presence and at God's voice, but Moses assured them with these words:

Moses said to the people, "Do not be afraid; for God has come in order to test you, and in order that the fear of Him may remain with you, so that you may not sin." Exodus 20:20

In this story we find something interesting taking place. The children of Israel reacted to God in fearfulness, and they *ran from His presence.* But Moses responded to God in fear, and he *ran into His presence.* The key difference is that the genuine fear of God will draw us to Him, not drive us away from Him. This is why God said,

He made known his ways to Moses, His acts to the sons of Israel. Psalm 103:7

The fear of the Lord helps us to know Who God is and not just what God can do.

4. That the people would obey what God said.

God has given us commandments – not suggestions. His plan and intent is for His people to obey His Word. We bring trouble and danger upon ourselves through our disobedience. Listen to these words penned by John Kilpatrick:

Church, let me caution you. Get outside the perimeter of the Word of God and you get outside the perimeter of the Blood. Once this happens, it's easy to be swayed by evil doctrines and evil men. It may look good, sound good, feel good and even seem good, but it may not be God. Be alert. Do not be deceived. The first thing that happens during a revival is that the devil will come with a strong spirit of deception (Kilpatrick, 1995, p. 120).

The prophet Samuel confronted King Saul by telling him *"to obey is better than sacrifice" (1 Samuel 15:22).* In those days sacrifice was a sign of commitment and a form of worship. Samuel told Saul that obedience to God and His Word was the highest form of worship offered to Him. James reiterates this truth by calling us to *"be doers of the word and not hearers only" (James 1:22)*. Our obedience to God's Word shows the level to which we value what He has said.

James continues by saying,

But one who looks intently at the perfect law, the law of liberty, and abides by it, not having become a forgetful hearer but an effectual doer, this man will be blessed in what he does. James 1:25

God desires that we value His Word. He wants us to hear from Him, to learn from Him, to have a healthy fear of Him, and to be obedient to Him. As our focus stays on God's Word, we will see God continue to move in our lives and to bring His blessing and His favor.

Maintaining Accountability

Then Shaphan brought the book to the king and reported further word to the king, saying, "Everything that was entrusted to your servants they are doing."

We discussed in Chapter Eight the importance of delegation. I stressed how valuable it is for people to be given responsibility and authority. In addition, people need to be given boundaries and to be held accountable. While King Josiah entrusted others to do the work brought about by revival, there was still accountability in place. As the repair of the temple was being accomplished, the progress was reported back to him. Checks and balances were in place, and everyone was accountable to someone. Accountability provides a form of protection and care, establishing boundaries and unity that can never be realized in isolation.

The value of teamwork cannot be overstated. We need one another. Even as Jesus was training His disciples for ministry, He sent them out "two by two" (Mark 6:7). In the midst of revival, it is very dangerous for people to become isolated or to function outside of any level of accountability. A move of God can quickly be interrupted by surprises or by a lack of communication. Keep the lines of communication clear, and the elements of accountability in place, to ensure and protect the move of God.

There is strength in accountability and in being connected to others in Christ. When done properly, accountability provides mutual edification and growth. Consider this powerful truth from Ecclesiastes:

And if one can overpower him who is alone, two can resist him. A cord of three strands is not quickly torn apart.
Ecclesiastes 4:12

I encourage you to be wise, and to be willing to partner with other believers in accountability, and to *"spur one another on toward love and good deeds" (Hebrews 10:24).*

In the midst of revival it can be so easy to focus on superstars. Yet God is looking for servants, and God has made you to be that servant. As we allow God to use us as He has made us, we will see great things done both in our lives as well as through our lives. Add to that a proper emphasis on God's Word and the parameters of proper accountability and you have the ingredients in place to experience a powerful move of God.

Conclusion

Revival is Productive

"Everything that was entrusted to your servants they are doing." 2 Chronicles 34:16

Shaphan reported to King Josiah that everything was being done as requested and the people were faithfully doing the work of God. The price was being paid, order was being restored, and the temple was being repaired. The death that had been brought upon a nation through years of disobedience and evil was now being replaced with life as they were doing what was right in the eyes of the Lord. With things in the proper order, true productivity was taking place. At its core revival is productive.

I was in a group coaching session with Sam Farina and he introduced the following concept, which sums up what we have been exploring throughout this book. God has established an order that will be effective and productive – if we follow it.

Relationships – Roles – Responsibilities – Results

As we allow relationships to be our foundation – both our relationship with God and our relationship with others – the things we want to see happen will happen. Everything that God has written and spoken to us is founded on relationship. Out of the proper prioritizing of relationship, our roles become established. When we understand the relationship that we are in, we know what our roles are within the context of that relationship. By knowing what our roles are, it will clarify our responsibilities. It is much easier to know what to do when you know who you are. Finally, when this order is followed, the results will take care of themselves.

In our foundational passage (2 Chronicles 34), we find Josiah being placed on the throne at the age of eight, thus putting him on course for the fulfillment of his prophetic destiny (see 1 Kings 13:1-3). We discover that throughout his life and his reign as king, God helped him become what He had planned. As he followed the ways of God and walked in the godly heritage of his father David, he fulfilled his godly destiny. He learned the value of reigning over sin, and of leading and sustaining a revival in the land. Through his leadership this revival brought purging throughout the land as it spread beyond its origin in Jerusalem. By doing what was right in the eyes of the Lord, Josiah reigned for thirty-one years.

As Josiah dealt aggressively with sin and saw the spread of revival, the work and responsibility also spread and increased. Josiah grew in his trust for God, his trustworthiness to God, and his ability to trust others with responsibility. As the work increased, so did the need for laborers and delegation. Everyone was willing to pay the price to accomplish much for God's Kingdom. Encouragement and accountability were instituted to better facilitate the work of God. As Josiah allowed people to serve the Lord out of their gifts and abilities, and as God's Word was kept as a priority, God's blessing and favor were realized.

While the reign of Josiah did not erase the problems and wickedness of the past, it did bring the children of Israel back to a proper focus during that time. 2 Chronicles 34 closes out with these words:

Josiah removed all the abominations from all the lands belonging to the sons of Israel, and made all who were present in Israel to serve the LORD their God. Throughout his lifetime they did not turn from following the LORD God of their fathers. 2 Chronicles 34:33

Throughout the life and reign of Josiah the people did not turn from following the Lord. What a powerful statement to be made about him and his reign.   This is a wonderful example of someone leading a revival. My prayer is that God would once again raise up men and women like Josiah who would by example lead people back to the ways of the Lord.

As we faithfully apply the principles from this book in our lives, we too will see God's blessing and favor realized. Whether you are in revival or not, these principles are important in providing the structure for revival. May the torch for revival that we carry burn bright and strong to bring about impact and change in our lives and our world. May God pour out His Spirit in and through our lives both now and forever!

Restore us, O God of our salvation, and cause Your indignation toward us to cease. Will You be angry with us forever? Will You prolong Your anger to all generations? Will You not Yourself revive us again, that Your people may rejoice in You? Show us Your lovingkindness, O LORD, and grant us Your salvation. Psalm 85:4-7

Bibliography

Brown, D. M. (1993). *The End of the American Gospel Enterprise.* Shippensburg: Destiny Image Publishers.

Cecil Robeck, J. (2006). *The Azusa Street Mission and Revival.* Nashville: Thomas Nelson.

Duewel, W. (1995). *Revival Fire.* Grand Rapids: Zondervan.

Hill, S. (1997). *White Cane Religion.* Shippensburg: Destiny Image Publishers.

Kilpatrick, J. (1995). *Feast of Fire.* Pensacola: Brownsville Assembly of God.

Ravenhill, L. (1979). *Why Revival Tarries.* Bloomington: Bethany House Publishers.